AS I SAW IT

KEITH WELLS

AS I SAW IT

KEITH WELLS

This book contains references to real stories about real people, most of which are not identified by their real names, and in many cases, persons' roles, positions, or titles have been changed to protect the actual identity of the persons depicted in the stories. All of the events and stories in the book are a product of the author's remembrance and interpretation of these events, which might vary slightly from the actual event.

Copyright @ 2022 by Keith Wells

ISBN: 979-8-360-70734-9

Acknowledgments

Graphic Design .... Debbie Wilson
Cover Artisit .... Rebecca Selfe
Inspiration to Write .... Michael Palmer
Publishing Advisor .... Peter Davidson
Reader .... Robert Jackson

DEDICATED TO

Scott J. Wells
Susan E. Hunt

Table of Contents

Chapter 1 Childhood

How I Came To Be 1
My Early Experience With Women 2
Three and a Half Blocks of Hell 4
Train Tracks 5

Chapter 2 Ireton

An Introduction To Ireton 11
Geographic Ireton 19
Wells Store 22
Pheasant Hunting in Iowa 24
Scoby Hall 26

Chapter 3 Navy

It Was San Diego After All 31
Sea The World 33
Life on Treasure Island 39
My First Cruise To San Francisco 41
A Trip To The Top 43
Revenge 45
Austin Healey Sprite 47
Ship in Dry Dock 49
The Purple Onion 50
Woman Love 51
Coffee House in San Diego 52
Tijuana Taxi 54
Balboa 56
Ocean Beach is Now Dog Beach 60

Chapter 4 Chicago

A Visit To Chicago 63
Carol's Family 66
How About You, You Want a Piece of Me? 68

Chapter 5 Boulder

Indian Peaks Burial Ground 71
From Boulder to Richmond 73

Chapter 6 Okoboji

22 Orchard Lane 77
Horner's Stories 81
The Poets Club 83

Chapter 7 Albuquerque

It Shouldn't Happen To A Dog 87
The First Time Is The Hardest 89
A Friend in Need 93
Dan From PWP 95
Ruby's Country Bar 96

Chapter 8 Guadalajara

ITESM 101

Chapter 9 Tucson

Jeep Tour Guide 107
Living Under a Bridge in Tucson 110

Chapter 10 Single Again

Treading On Thin Ice 111
Melaque Was Beautiful Nevertheless 113
Yacht Club 116

Chapter 11 Travels

Some Tips on Baby Care.....................119
Traveling With Lurch........................123
Second Half of My Early Retirement Trip.........126
Cruise to Santa Catalina......................131
Healdsburg Wine Tour........................132
Smokin' Up Highway 1.......................134
The Red Van Trip............................139
Burros Love Dave............................142
My Last RV Trip.............................144

Chapter 12 Life Changing Decision

Accounting? Really?..........................151
I May Have Done It This Time................153
Insignificant Decisions With Life Changing Results...155

Chapter 13 Jobs & Investments

High Paying Jobs I Haven't Had................159
Buy High, Sell Low..........................162
How Did That Summers Off Thing Work Out For You..163
My First Class Taught at a University............164
Teaching at Edgewood.......................166

Chapter 14 Thought & Opinions

Music Man..................................169
Boredom...................................172
Gardening and Other Loves...................174
When Did Health Become The Main Topic of Discussion.177
Would That Look Better If....................178
My Affection For Cars.......................182
Crazy Teachers.............................185
The Twenty Minute Window..................188

Chapter 1
Childhood

How I Came To Be

Contrary to popular belief, I was not just a mistake even though my siblings were 15 and 17 years old when I was born. I wasn't even in school yet when my brother left for WWII.

The story goes that in the 1930's in Iowa if a divorced woman could not declare a support source the State would step in and put the kids in an orphanage. This happened to my first cousin who was now in her twenties.

The family had an intervention to determine what could be done about her two very young children, a girl and a boy. My parents decided that they would take the little two-year old girl to raise. Another family member took the boy.

After three years of raising the little girl, the mother appeared at the door and wanted the child back. Since no adoption papers had been drawn up, there was no option but to give her up.

My parents were so distraught they decided to have their own little girl to replace her. Only I was a boy. I was told by my sister that they dressed me in left over girl clothes until I outgrew them.

So, at 50 and 39 my parents, with two kids in high school,

Keith Wells

decide to have a baby, and here I am. I grew up with being the age of my second cousins. Every where we went, I was always the youngest person there.

Now at 82, everywhere I go I am always the oldest. What a rude turn around!

My Early Experience With Women

Having a new kid arrive was pretty special when there were only six other kids my age living in town and I had yet to meet five of them. It was especially nice having a playmate move in directly across the street. Kind of small I thought, but then she was a girl and only three years old. I felt quite worldly at four years old introducing her to all the sights of that square block. Most intriguing was of course the baseball diamond. The dugouts were favorite hideaways. A huge thicket that bordered her grandmother's property had a special hideout I had made. Then there was the other side of the alley where the obnoxious 12 year old, Walt, had a pigeon house and two huge trees that would later accommodate a tree house.

Old Walt taught us a lot of very interesting things not the least of which was how to strike a match to light a cigarette butt without burning your hands. The ball park bleachers across the street provided an excellent cigarette butt supply which Walt kept in a coffee can in the pigeon pen. Later I would become sole owner of the can and supply the kids I had not yet met. Little wonder I was the smallest boy in class. Then again, there were only five of us including the farm boys. Twelve girls though. Good odds I always thought.

Walt educated us on many facets of nature. We learned about how to identify different types of pigeons, how to repair my broken wagon, the fine art of attaching roller skates to street

As I Saw It

shoes and a bit of anatomy. I became acutely aware that Jen and I had some distinct differences. I'm convinced that unlike me Walt knew Jen was built missing some parts. He told us that part A actually fit into part B! Can you imagine! Likely old Walt would have gotten a few years in the slammer for that lesson. There were more constructive things Walt taught us that a 4 and a 3 year old could do to amuse yourselves like peeing through a dandelion stem, which by the way was considerably more easy for me than the very frustrated Jen. This may have been the origin of penis envy. I suppose today we'd have been in therapy for years, but in those days it was considered part of growing up. Later when I met some of the boys from seven blocks way across town I found out that much wilder and more perverse things happened over there.

One of the more private passions Jen and I had was playing cowboys. Naturally cowboys had camp fires and Walt kept us indirectly supplied with matches in the coffee can. One not so famous session of playing cowboys, Jen and I built a small campfire down near the ballpark outhouse. We carried leaves from the thicket all the way down to our campsite. I'd watched Dad burn leaves on the gravel roadside by our house, so it wasn't as though I was a novice. What I hadn't counted on was how fire spread much faster on the nearby dead grass than it did on gravel roads!

It didn't take long for me to figure out I had to run up to our cistern for some water. Jen hightailed it for home. Pumping water was strictly forbidden when your cistern was the sole source of water for the whole house. My mother came running out to see what had possessed me to break the forbidden rule. The fire was about half way to the new bleachers when the volunteer fire department arrived. Thankfully no structures were burned, only dry grass.

Keith Wells

I did get a good bit of recognition around the little town thereafter. I heard more than one person say "there's the little brat that tried to burn down the ball park." The uproar more or less subsided by the time I entered first grade two years later.

Jen's mother became quite famous for being the first to announce and celebrate the end of WWII. One afternoon she ran over to our house and had my mom and I pile into her car. She drove down town to our block and a half Main Street where she honked the horn while we all hollered "the war is over." That would be with Germany, not Japan.

When the second part of the war ended, Jen and her mother joined her dad, who had been in the Army. They moved to a town seventeen miles away. I was devastated. It was like a five year old's divorce! I started to meet some of the other town kids after the war, but I basically had little to do with "women friends" for the next ten years.

Three and a Half Blocks of Hell

The Ireton school was three and a half blocks from our house. On the way there was a hill that became perilous for me from first grade on. I was six; John was about twelve. Every time he caught me going to or from school he would terrorize the devil out of me.

It started with his damnable dog. This mutt got two joys out of life; chasing kids and chasing cars. He didn't have much luck with cars but he caught me several times and would nip at my ankles. Don't remember him drawing much blood but he could sure traumatize a kid.

One day when the dog was chasing me I swung around and kicked him. John happened to see this and from that day on both of them delighted in terrorizing me. John would beat me up any

As I Saw It

chance he got. A beating up in those days usually meant one or two punches in an arm or mid section, never any blood. My parents knew of this dilemma but back then kids had to work out problems with other kids themselves.

On one particular lunch hour I was on my way back to school from lunch at home when old John caught me and gave me a punch or two. I was sort of sniffing as I approached the school when my older cousin Meryl saw me and asked why I was crying. I told him about my travails with John. Meryl said come on over here and sit on the hill by the light pole and let's wait for John.

As girls Meryl knew approached he asked them to sit with us. When John approached, Meryl grabbed him, made him climb up on the second rung of this light pole; ripped his pants down as he climbed, then whacked him on the ass about half a dozen times while all the girls were laughing their butts off.

When the girls moved on, Meryl let John come down. He grabbed him by the shoulders and said, "you see that kid sitting over there, he's my cousin, and if you ever touch him again I'll beat you to a bloody pulp."

John had little reason not to believe Meryl couldn't do so because his older brother was a Golden Gloves boxing champion for the Navy and used Meryl and his brothers as sparing partners. Everyone in town pretty much new better than to mess with any of those brothers.

Life became much easier after that. If John ever saw me he would cross the street to be sure I wasn't feeling threatened. Now all I had to contend with was that damned dog.

Train Tracks

My wanderlust started in that third grade class gazing out an open window at the pastoral view of my escape route from

Keith Wells

boredom - the railroad tracks east out of Ireton, Iowa.

I counted the minutes until 3:05 p.m. when the steam engine pulled out of town going east with it's one passenger car, one mail car, one freight car and that glorious red caboose.

I would watch the smoke pouring out of that magical steam engine and be carried away to those wonderful places it must be headed far beyond. Places where my mother had taken me on that same train every summer to visit my grandparents in southern Missouri. Two of the mystical places for me were the Omaha and Kansas City train stations.

It was on a late connecting train transfer on the train from Omaha to Kansas City that I saw my first black man. Mom was dragging our huge suitcase toward the train platform when a porter picked me up in one arm and the bag in his other hand. Needless to say I was shocked not only of being hoisted up and being carried running toward the door but to be within inches of this man's nearly coal black face sported by a bright red cap with a bill like policemen wear. My instinct was to push away and holler "Mom! He's burnt!" My mother was so embarrassed and apologized profusely to this poor gentleman. He sat me down beside our train-car and said "Lady, it's alright, I have heard much worse."

Train stations continued to fascinate me with their bright lights, wooden benches, grand restaurants and the majestic restrooms with urinals taller than my head. I would slip away from my mother as often as I could on the pretense of having to "go" so I could stop and watch those wonderful old black men shining rich men's shoes. I imagined myself some day sitting up on one of those thrones having my shoes shined.

My mother's sister-in-law changed that notion in one instant one day when she refused to serve food to a similar old black man in her diner. It was then in the 1950's that I became acutely

As I Saw It

aware of the struggle that black people were living through. That awareness was reinforced when in 1963 on an interview trip with Delta Airlines a black man in his 60's opened a door for me and called this twenty-three year old "sir."

I was not a farm kid as most of my Ireton friends were. My father owned a general store. You could buy cookies that were in a bulk box that people took out with their fingers, vinegar that came out of a barrel, eggs that I personally candled in the earth floor basement and men's work clothes. Personal items, as Dad called them, (Kotex) had to be individually wrapped in green paper so as not to embarrass his women customers. Of course everyone in the town of 350 people knew exactly what was inside those distinctively green paper wrapped boxes.

Since kids clothing wasn't sold in Ireton, every fall I had to get school clothes out of town. Usually JC Penny's in Hawarden the metropolis of 1,200 people nine miles away. On one occasion my parents put me on a bus to Sioux City to shop for my first high school clothes. I got two pair of Levis with buttons, for $3.50 each. Dad got calls from disgusted parents who complained that "he had spent so much money on these fancy pants and now their kids wanted them. Your store sold work pants, were they not good enough for your kid? Your pants are only $2.50." How dare he!

A senior class trip to Minneapolis sealed the deal, I was a city kid. In a small mid-western town mostly controlled by one church very few entertaining things happen. There were no movie theaters allowed in town and no high school dances. The only dance in Ireton was one my buddy and I put on by renting the town hall for $25 and providing music with a 45 record player. It was a smash hit. Andy the town hall custodian warned me that we would be in trouble. I hadn't expected the closed minded people to call my father to complain about me leading the town's

Keith Wells

kids straight into the depths of hell.

We boys counted the days until we could get a license to drive so we could run over to Hawarden where they had drive in theaters, drive in restaurants and even an indoor movie theater. It was even rumored that Hawarden had a whore house. A red lightbulb shown on the second floor of a building on Main Street. We used to drive quickly up the alley just to look at that red bulb. I never heard a single bit of evidence that it was indeed a house of ill repute. Years later when I brought my Chicago girlfriend to meet my mother, her comment after seeing many of my friends with kids said "what Ireton needed was a theater."

Immediately upon graduating from high school my escape plan went into full mode. I joined the US Navy. Being sent to boot camp in San Diego surrounded by palm trees, an ocean, and beautiful warm weather in December was like heaven. I enjoyed nearly every minute I spent in San Diego.

San Francisco for electronic school was even more exotic. Subsequent visits via destroyer Navy ship to Hawaii, Midway Island, Formosa (now Taiwan), Japan and Hong Kong gave me all the excitement I had been craving, and then some! I do not recommend extended cruises on Navy destroyers no matter how bored you are.

On my first furlough home after being in the Western Pacific I was shocked that the conversation after five minutes with my old buddies was whether or not rain would come next week. Also after drinking underage in California for three years I was finally carded while in uniform at a little shit bar in Hudson, SD where we had gone to play pool for all four years of high school! I asked the owner, "don't you recognize me? I have been coming here for years!"

Now and then I hear a train whistle on one of the golf courses I play and I hark back to those innocent days of the third grade

As I Saw It

and wonder where my life would have taken me if I had not had a view of the railroad tracks.

Keith Wells

Chapter 2
Ireton

An Introduction To Ireton

Looking back on it, growing up in beautiful downtown Ireton was quite special and I don't mean the Southerner's connotation of special which loosely translated means rider on the short bus. People in Iowa did some really crazy stuff back in the 40's and 50's. Not like current Florida crazy, but then again many Floridians came from Iowa! Many really happy times occurred there followed by long periods of sheer boredom.

One of great things about Ireton was that you were only nine miles from Hawarden. Hawarden was where all the real action occurred. My god they even had a drive in cafe right on Highway 10 as you came into town. One of life's great moments was when you were actually old enough to go to the drive in by yourself. Like I said, life was pretty simple in a town of 350 people. One of my buddies would not date Ireton girls, only Hawarden girls. The Hawarden kids didn't seem to mind but it sure pissed off a lot of Ireton girls. He was quite handsome.

When you are pretty much in charge of your own entertainment things can get pretty creative. Take roadside skiing for instance. Some one would tow you on a long rope while you

Keith Wells

were on skis in a snowy roadbed. Quite a trick to keep between gravel and a barbed wire fence. That was a black rated slope in the flatlands of Iowa. My buddy Todd and his sister Kate were the main instigators of this sport since they had the only pair of skis in town.

Haunted houses were always a favorite. More farmers were abandoning their farm houses and moving into our booming metropolis. We even had the beginnings of a suburb down along the rail road tracks east of town soon after I left for the Navy. I was so glad that occurred while I was away and not in the third grade where I would daydream of travel while looking out at those tracks running east from town. Those wonderful tracks would not be visible from the third grade window. Of course it wouldn't matter because the train had stopped running years ago. It didn't matter anyhow, I already had the travel bug.

My favorite haunted house was about three miles southwest of town. It was ungodly creepy around ten at night. On this particular night the decoy, Hank, had been sent ahead to hide and jump out to scare the hell out the girls we had talked into going out there. Once there, the eight of us creeped around over broken pieces of wood, broken glass, flattened card board boxes and scattered old clothes. Hank was hiding in the closet of the second bedroom upstairs. When all eight of us were in the room, Hank jumped out of the closet screaming bloody murder! Kate, the first girl in high school to develop boobs, was standing right beside me. She let out this blood curdling scream and jumped onto me with legs and arms surrounding me. I was so grateful. It was my first feel of boobs although it was through two shirts and two coats. Heavenly! That is as close as I ever got to actually touching them, but it was a lasting memory.

The one and only gas station in Ireton was kind of a meeting place for the Ireton boys. It had a 5 cent bottled coke machine

As I Saw It

and a penny peanut machine. Kind of a pre-McDonald's for Ireton, which to this date still does not have a McDonald's. I worked at this Skelly gas station which was owned by my high school girlfriend's brother Dave. That wasn't a factor in obtaining the job, I was just one of the only boys in town. Much important information would be shared at Skelly's, such as who will be available for outhouse tipping on Halloween or watermelon stealing on the weekend. Many tales were exchanged of who probably was doing whom around town. I didn't publicize the fact that very likely I was the person who had the inside track on that information. Why? Because I often had more condom customers in my evening shift than I had customers for gasoline. Coin Pacs, they were called. The vernacular in those days was "rubbers." They we're individually wrapped in gold fold and sold at fifty cents for a three pack. I didn't become top rubber salesman in Sioux County by design.

A gent in a suit came in one afternoon and asked for Dave. I explained that Dave's wife was expecting and he was home attending to her. He said that's ok, I will just check his desk. I said "I don't think so and you had better leave." Later that day I saw him talking and laughing with Dave. Dave called me aside later and gave me a lesson on rubbers including rolling one out to show me how it would be put on lest a perspective customer needed education as well. Dave cautioned me that these were never to be used on his sister. Considering the birth rate in that county, I would have expected he would have suggested the opposite.

When word got out to the horny boys from Ireton (and several towns around) that they could get Coin Pacs from this 16 year old kid with no questions asked, sales picked up tenfold. Frequently these lads would pull into the single car pull through with their prospective love interest sitting beside them with an

Keith Wells

embarrassed face looking straight down at the floor board. Thus I came to know who was buying rubbers for use on whom almost nightly. Dave asked me one day if I could possibly use my sales ability to try to improve the sale of gas.

Outhouse tipping was a very important ritual in the 50's. Amazing how many folks still had them. We did until I was fifteen, but my wise old father had the foresight to pay the extra bucks to have ours bolted to a cement foundation. Others in town, not so lucky. One in particular belonged to this crusty old bastard who lived next door to Dan and his little brother. This boastful twit came down to Skelly's on the afternoon on Halloween saying to Dave, "those son's of bitches aren't gonna tip my outhouse tonight cause I gotter wired down and I'll be inside with my shotgun." My boss just looked at me and I turned away. This was like candy to a baby! How could he not know I was a part of this! There were only about half a dozen boys that lived in town!

Dan's little brother posted guard. It gets cold in Iowa in the fall. Mr Crusty, the outhouse sentinel, and his trusty shotgun had to go in for coffee and to warm up. Word was quickly conveyed to Dan, Rod and me that it was time for action. We were waiting with a farm-grade fencing wire cutter a half a block away between two stores on Main Street. Rod, being the most skilled in fencing, clipped the wire and held the pieces together with a thin piece of stove pipe wire so the cut would not be noticed. We were waiting for the armed guard to re-enter his post. When we were certain he was seated all three of us hit the back side of that outhouse with full force tipping it onto the door which locked our ungracious host inside. I, being tallest, was in the center. It went over so fast I lost my footing and slipped down. Had I not grabbed hold of the planking underneath and pulled myself up, I would have been waist deep in shyste! We went scurrying back

As I Saw It

to our hiding place and peaked out. By then Crusty had his head sticking through one of the holes and was screaming "you sons of bitches, I'll get you for this!"

How we became familiar with shotguns for use other than pheasants and outhouse guarding was by way of rock salt. Farmers would open the ends of shotgun shells, pour out the BBs and fill the casings with rock salt. This would supposedly sting the water melon thief without serious injuries. I like to think that I was far too swift of foot to ever have that experience. One of my buddies, Jim, and I did experience what I thought was much more threatening than rock salt when we were lifting a couple of choice small melons from a farm west of town. We had crossed a pasture to get to a garden where the melons were. As we were leaving with our "borrowed" produce in hand, Jim said "run!" I heard it too, a horse's hooves. How the hell were we to know a horse would chase sounds in the dark! I didn't even know this guy HAD a horse much less that it might chase you at night! We quickly came upon the barbed wire fence. There was no time to climb back over so I dived and slid under it. Apparently Jim didn't see the fence and hit it dead center with a sproing! He was able to slide under before the horse just sort of moseyed up to the fence and looked at us. I was most afraid of what might be on top of that horse with his rock salt weapon. Nothing tho, just horse. I was told that Jim had several chest and thigh scars from barbs piercing his skin.

Hunting was a big attraction in NW Iowa and SW South Dakota. I started training early with my older brother's BB gun that had the stock broken off. I was hell on birds. Not something I am proud of now but I guess the hunter instinct came naturally. My father sure didn't encourage it. I think he'd had quite enough shooting in the invasion of a France in WWI. His army rifle and scared up helmet up in the attic looked like he'd been to hell and

Keith Wells

back. Fishing wasn't an interest he held either. I cultivated that talent on my own as I did hunting.

One morning when I was about seven, I was out front with this broken BB gun when three teenagers came by. They were laughing at me and my sorry looking weapon. One said "I'll give you a nickel if you can hit that bird over on the line." I promptly picked it off like nothing. They walked away shaking their heads. I said "where's my nickel?" They said "get lost kid." I think that was the beginning of my distrust of braggarts.

My prowess with hunting changed from birds to rabbits and pheasants at about ten. I knew a lot of farmers who encouraged me to come out and shoot pesky pigeons off their barns with my new BB gun. The local lumberyard welcomed me as well to do away with sparrows that pooped on their nice clean boards. This would become a big help when I later would ask farmers to walk their fields for pheasant hunting. They knew by then I was very safety conscious and would not mistake one of their cows for a pheasant.

My transition from BB gun to rifle and shotgun was facilitated by a dairy half block from my house. As a small kid I loved to go over at milking time to watch. I knew all eight cows by name and some of them would come to me when called. It was a gang ritual for newcomers to be asked to pee on the electric fence without getting zapped. All rural kids would know to listen for the click to know when the jolt would be sent, right? Well not little Pete! The jolt knocked him back and probably stunted his wiennie growth for life!

The dairy owner had the most fascinating gun that he used to shoot rats in his barn. It was a double barrel but not in the classic sense. It had a .22 rifle on top with a .410 shotgun underneath. After much cajoling I convinced the owner to let me borrow it from time to time to hunt rabbits and pheasants. After nearly filling a freezer with these delicacies, my father relented and bought me my own .22 and later a shotgun. They more than paid for themselves in a constant supply of meat. If you have not tried rabbit or pheasant you have missed a real midwestern treat.

As my age group of boys got older the newest recreation became parking with your girl friend for serious necking and petting. It never got beyond that for me but I have several friends with "older kids" who can attest to the fact that more than necking was going on out on the dirt road east of town called Lovers Lane. It was famous for other things as well. One of the farm owners on that road had a stack of hay bales right against the road. Because some of the dozen or so of male friends in high school took great exception to the farmer not allowing any of his three very attractive daughters to date anyone of us, it was decided that his haystack needed moving. Eleven of us moved it to the middle of Lovers Lane in about six minutes flat. Next day in study hall our superintendent came in, selected eleven of us and said, "get your asses out there and move that haystack right now." Interestingly he missed by only one; he picked one guy who was not there and missed one who was. Naturally I was selected.

Our town cop was a story unto himself. His name was Phil. His son Rick was a friend of mine. Kind of wild in my estimation, but nevertheless a one year older friend. Rick was the only person who ever took me for a ride in 1956 Plymouth at 120 miles per hour on the way to Hawarden. I truly needed that coke at the local drive-in when we arrived in record time. (That speed would not be repeated until the 1980's when I owned a Nissan 300Z.) Rick's dad would kindly look the other way when I would drive by him at 14 or 15 years old.

Try as Phil might he could not discourage the outhouse tipping group. On the night of Mr Crusty's tipping, Phil actually drove me home twice. I think he was a bit perturbed that he had

Keith Wells

to help upright that outhouse and rescue its inhabitant. After the first ride home, I almost beat Phil back downtown. On the second trip an hour later Phil said in his Dutch accent, "Got dammit, I mean it this time Keet. I catch you again yura goin' 'ta jail." I respectfully waited a half hour or so before going back down town. I knew he wouldn't put me in the tiny cell in the city garage because it had several hundred pounds of fertilizer bags stored in it. Plus it was time for the news on TV; Phil would not miss the news for some minor misdemeanor.

Phil's assistant, Andy, was a very special case for the Ireton kids to harass. Probably we'd have ignored him if he didn't try so hard to be important. He even bought his own red light to sit on the dash of his dark blue Ford four door sedan when it was parked around the corner from the bowling alley on Main. One special occasion comes to mind. We posted watches on all the corners of Main, then one of the guys speeded past the window of the bowling alley where Andy was sitting, drinking coffee. My function was to report back to the group on Andy's reaction. It was really a hoot! He jumped up, spilled his coffee, and dashed out to his waiting "personal squad car." I ran out with him to report his reaction to us having lifted the car ever so slightly and setting cement blocks under the rear axel so when he jammed it into first gear, with his red light dutifully plugged into the cigarette lighter, the wheels just spun. Good thing Phil was on vacation, we might have pushed him over the limit on that one.

Celebrations were a big thing in Ireton especially Memorial Day and the Fourth of July where the whole town turned out in patriotic support of our veterans both living and deceased. I was a cadence drummer for the high school marching band. I had come up with a pretty lively rendition for our band and each Memorial Day our band would lead a group of vets up the two block long central avenue in Ireton's Memorial Cemetery.

As I Saw It

I thought I was quite inspiring as I drummed our band on my last march of my senior year. At the end of the avenue there was a circular memorial to deceased veterans. I did a special roll-off and brought the band to a halt. In a couple of minutes this old vet wheezed up to me and said, "Jesus kid, what the hell was the hurry? You damned near killed us old farts!" At my age now I definitely realize I may have jazzed it up a bit.

Geographic Ireton

The layout of Ireton in the 1950's was pretty simple: eight blocks square. If you were entering town on the gravel road west of the cemetery that would become a paved Main Street (tho there were no street signs anywhere, you just knew it was Main Street) you would first come to the Juffer house on the right. That first street to your right would run all the way east to the baseball field right across the street from the Wells home and Grau's Dairy.

Continuing north on Main the next street would be where the water tower sat with a one unit stone sided garage that held "thee city truck" and a metal lattice sided cell that was our city jail. I never heard of anyone spending a night there tho Phil, the town cop, threatened me with that on one outhouse tipping Halloween.

One block further would bring you to the Methodist Church where I attended, sang in the choir, read bible verses at service and contemplated becoming a Methodist minister by attending Morningside Methodist College in Sioux City. The combination of discovering beer, becoming enthralled with cars and girls (one in particular) and my father's untimely death changed all that.

One more block north would bring you to the beginning of our one block down town. The Corner Store (our competitor) and Satterley's Drug Store were across from each other. Next

Keith Wells

came my father's store, Wells Store and across the street was Pete's butcher shop. Pete's was famous for having a cat that lived in the store.

Further down the block was a tavern, a popcorn stand whose owner enticed young boys for immoral purposes with popcorn, a pool hall, another grocery store competitor whose daughter was a friend of mine, a lot for basket ball in the summer and hockey in the winter, the post office (our post box was number 2), and a farm product dealer who also sold propane.

At the beginning of the next block was Skelly Service Station where I worked as a 16 year old. Dave, the owner, was a brother to the only girl I dated in high school. The steep hill next to Skelly was closed for sledding in the winter. My cousin lived at the bottom of the hill. I would call upon her for cocoa on very cold days.

Across from Skelly Service was Lila's Beauty Shop, owner and mother of my oldest friend Rod whom I met at two years of age, tho I don't remember. Further down the block was our City Park. It had swings and a teeter-totter. Darel lived across the street from the park. His claim to fame was that he had some malady the caused his penis to be always erect, quite a fete in itself.

One block further north and you reached the lumberyard. Across from the lumberyard was our train depot. It actually had a waiting room where occasionally people like my mother and I would wait for the 3:05 to Omaha when we were off to visit my grand parents. I loved the smoking 3:05 steam engine. Behind the train depot was a creek where we would fish for the nonexistent big catch.

Now if you were entering Ireton from the north you would be on a blacktop road that came from Highway 10. First you would cross the railroad tracks, then drive halfway through town to a right turn that took you Main Street and the beginning of our

As I Saw It

"downtown."

The first block going west would end at the Christian Reform Church which dictated the town's morality. There would be no dancing nor any movies in town but screwing in the backseat was perfectly acceptable. My buddy Bruce and I put on the one and only town dance at the City Hall. We used a 45 record player. It was a monumental success, but my parents were besieged with complaints from The Christian Reform Church members. My fondest memory of the dance was when a friend of mine told my girl friend that the hard thing she may have felt when dancing with him was his pocket knife.

Next block was the entirety of Ireton Public School. Notice I said Public School, not just High School. First grade through eighth wason the first floor and high school had the second floor.

The following block was owned by Pete the town cop. His house across from the school had a pasture behind it which took up the rest of the block.

Next block going west had the City Hall, site of our library in the basement and the only dance ever put on upstairs. At the end of this block was Main Street. Just before the end was the old doctor's office in the 1940's where I got my first penicillin shot and a bakery which was short lived. Most women baked in those days.

The next block contained Sinkey Garage and a farm implements dealer on the left and Carl Braak's blacksmith shop on the right. Just beyond the implement dealer was an actual hitching post for horses. Carl's son Dan and I were friends. When we were in high school we bought leather motorcycle type jackets and were then considered real rebels.

The next two blocks contained the residential homes of the Bartlet's and the owner of the implement dealer. I had an occasion to date the implement dealer's daughter who was considered to

Keith Wells

be very perky.

At the end of this block the pavement turned to gravel which led out to the town dump. I spent many hours keeping the rat population down with my trusty Marlin lever action .22.

There you have it. Ireton in a nutshell in the 1940's and 1950's. I have always joked that Ireton had to change their sign from Population 350 to Population 349 when I left for the Navy.

Wells Store

As you walked into the front door of Wells Store you were greeted by the smell of fresh fruits on a long display case to your left and a long hardwood floor running straight back to the rear wall.

On your right was an old hardwood framed leather couch for Dad's lady customers to rest on while shopping, one of the only places to sit in downtown Ireton that was not a cafe or bar. Dad was very thoughtful of his lady shoppers. Beside the couch, and running down the right wall was canned coffee first, followed by canned vegetables, and then soups.

In the center of the isle was a long row of bulk cookies in glass cases followed by saltine and Ritz crackers. Across the isle from this and adjacent the fruit display case was a large three shelf free standing candy case which I learned to man on busy Saturdays when the farmers came to town to shop.

Right to the side of the candy case was a door leading down a dark stairway toward a single lightbulb hanging from the ceiling to light the way. In the dark dirt floor basement the egg handling and storage area was the only lighted area. This was also the snow shovel storage area. A single lightbulb hung inside a three pound coffee can with two smooth holes cut in it to hold eggs up to when you checked them for dark spots, i.e, fertilized eggs which had the be separated from those we sold from the many cases

As I Saw It

farmers brought in to trade for food. This process is or was called candling eggs.

Just beyond the basement door on the left side of the store was the two service counters behind which was all the jello, pudding, dry mixes, coffee beans and an old red coffee grinder. The first counter (always preferred by customers and clerks alike) had a long string hanging down from near the ceiling. This string and the roll of wrapping paper on a bar paper cutter were used to wrap an assortment of items such as sliced meat or clothing items.

In the middle of the dual service counter was and old time cash register with buttons and a crank handle. The rear service counter had our seldom used adding machine with a crank handle also. Beside it was a hand crank meat slicer which was used with bulk lunch meats we would bring from a refrigerator at the back wall.

Across from the front service counter was a huge front loading furnace for which we would bring up coal in a coal bucket from the dark back of the basement. Across from the rear service counter was the Old Home Bread rack which Red, our bread man, would faithfully fill each day on a route from Sioux City some forty miles away. Red would always take a few minutes to speak to me tho I was only six when he took our route.

On the right side of the rear of the store was our clothing and "lady's area." For the men we carried gloves, overalls, jeans and work socks. For the ladies there was bolts of cloth, cheese cloth, and Kotex that Dad carefully wrapped in green wrapping paper so as not to embarrass any of his "lady shoppers." Of course everyone in Ireton knew what was in the green wrapped boxes.

In the very far right corner of the store was Dad's old roll top desk complete with desk pad and dip pen. Dad would dip the pen in ink and flick the excess off onto a colorfully specked floor

Keith Wells

below.

In the far left of the store was all the soap and cleaning products, a huge ledger cabinet for recording (by hand) customer charges, an old time refrigerator for meats, a wash stand, and a flimsy door to the back storage area. In there were piles and plies of boxes of canned goods and a barrel for dispensing bulk vinegar into customer's own bottles.

Out the double back doors was a large deck that would have made a great loading dock except it wasn't reachable from the street. A few steps down and about 30 feet lead to our private, locked out house. Matilda and the Bowden girls, our clerks, would have no part of finding a customer from the pool hall, down two doors, in our outhouse.

As a child it was great fun to drop in on Dad at least once a day often to get a candy bar. When I got a little older I would run the candy bar, wait on customers, take phone orders, candle eggs and run down from school to the store at lunch so Dad would get a thirty minute lunch followed by my thirty minutes lunch.

I used to joke that I was 15 before I found out bananas were yellow since Dad took home all the produce too old to sell. I would be fifteen when Dad sold the store to one of our competitors. The store became a restaurant. I was setting in a booth on the exact spot where the Wells Store couch had sat when I received news that my Dad had died. I was 17.

Pheasant Hunting in NW Iowa

Some kids like baseball, some like basketball, I liked pheasant hunting, and if I say so myself, I was pretty darn good at it. It started at ten when I would borrow the dairy farmer's over and under .410 and dash out to the rail road tracks east of town and hunt until I got too cold. I was just ten when I got my first pheasant.

As I Saw It

My prowess improved as did the quality of shotguns I bought thereafter. My first shotgun was a bolt action .410. It was light weight and made a great roadside gun when you scouted around the two lane gravel or dirt roads to find a likely spot for birds, (pheasants) then you hopped out of the car to flush them out.

I lugged around a heavy old 12 gauge lever action shot gun for a while but found it too clumsy to be of much use. My favorite became an automatic action 20 gauge which I used all of my teen years until I left for the Navy. God knows what happened to it when I left!

My older brother liked to come pick me up early on a Saturday morning to take me around hunting with him and a friend or two from Sioux City. I liked to think it was because of my keen hunting instincts but I suspect it was because I was their key to getting into the fields of farmers who knew me.

Pheasant hunting ceased for about twenty years until I returned to Northwestern Iowa to teach. Very quickly I met several avid pheasant hunters one of which insisted I buy a shotgun to go on the annual opening day in November. He took me to a little out of the way town named Sibley where there was a very small gun shop. I settled on an Ithaca pump 12 gauge, with bottom ejection. What a hoot! I'd never seem a shotgun eject a spent shell out the bottom. Don't know what advantage that would be, but it was very slick.

That Ithaca was incredible. I seldom missed a shot. At times I felt sorry for the pheasants. By this time I was married and had Scott and Susan. Since we were living in some of the world's best pheasant hunting area I thought it would be good to instill this favorite pass time in him. So I took him out west of Estherville for a little roadside hunting one day. He would have been eight or nine.

When I found a likely spot we carefully slipped under the

Keith Wells

fence and walked less than ten yards when a large male took off in a flurry. It is a startling thing when they take off because they often wait until they are right underfoot. My reaction was so quick I shot him before he reached much altitude at all. Usually they fly at about 45 degrees, hit a peak height, then glided back to a new hiding place on the ground.

I don't think Scott knew I was capable of moving so quickly and when the bird catapulted into the ground about ten yards away I think Scott was really traumatized. When we got home and he watched me clean this bird and pull out its beautiful feathers he got this sick look on his face, turned and walked away.

Pheasant hunting has never been discussed again.

Skoby Hall

The fall of 1957 was a tough year for me. My dad had died very unexpectedly and I was thrust into male head of the household in my senior year of high school. Mom was one of those "leave it to the man" types so she did not know how to drive, stoke a coal furnace, repair anything mechanical and had never written a check in her life. So suddenly I was the chauffeur for Mom and a widowed aunt in the same fix, household caretaker (I even had a pass to leave high school to stoke our home furnace) and we got a crash course in check writing from the local banker.

A lot of decisions had to be made as to post high school plans. Mom wanted to sell the house for college money, but I foofooed that idea and joined the Navy just days after graduation. I was sent to an induction center where much to my dismay they sent me home saying I had low blood pressure and was anemic. Go back home, take some vitamins and come back in six months they said. A more astute person would have accepted that "get out of jail card" and ran with it.

I decided in my senior year to do a correspondence course in

As I Saw It

airline work that some fast talking traveling salesmen talked my mom and I into. Dad would never have suckered into that deal. Just as I was finishing, a decision had to be made of where to go for on-site training, requiring more money of course. Hollywood, FL was the selection but as the date approached my cousin who had attended South Dakota State College in Brookings convinced me to try a semester there. I should have questioned why HE was not still enrolled!

The $35 speeding ticket on the way up should have been enough of an omen but I enrolled and went into my first dorm room. That placement was short lived because my room mate was a complete ass. My new roommate would be this lad from a ranch in western Wyoming. The closest town to their ranch was 30 miles so needless to say he was not very worldly. I got him his first date with a high school friend who wound up in the same college.

My dorm was called Skoby Hall. I still have a picture of me sitting at my desk in the uniform of the day, a white tee shirt with rolled up sleeves. Skoby Hall was just about five blocks from the college hangout bar. My roommate didn't know much about girls but he sure knew his beer! We spent a disproportionate amount of time down there. This was an old west bar and I soon found out there was one stool at the bar that was reserved for one blind guy. He knew exactly how to get to the bar and just how many steps to take to get to "his stool."

SDSC would become my first dabbling in golf. I signed up for it as a P.E. requirement. I must admit I didn't learn much in that class, but I could drive a ball a heck of a lot farther than I can now. It was in that gym that I learned the fine art of providing a urine sample. I didn't do it, but I watched a couple of guys pour beer into the specimen bottles.

It didn't take long to recognize that my desired Business major

Keith Wells

was going to face a lot of obstacles. First there was no Business major so I was put in as an Economics major. Secondly there were no other proposed Business majors there. Third this was an agriculture and engineer school and most of the boys ran around with slide-rules hanging from their belts. And lastly, neither I nor my timid roommate seemed to fit in. So I decided it was time to re-try the Navy.

I was going to go back to St. Louis where I was first rejected but I made a quick trip to see my old high school girlfriend. After an all night drive to see her I found she had been sleeping with a new boyfriend so off I went to the Navy recruiting station in St. Louis where this time I passed the health exam with flying colors. I also learned not to watch a blood draw; it can make you pretty queasy.

Since the airlines were on strike, the Navy sent three of us on a train to San Diego for boot camp. San Diego was one of two requirements I had before signing the dotted line. The other was a trade school. I'd chosen electronics technician school which would be in San Francisco after boot camp.

The train trip was memorable. The three of us headed straight for the bar car where we were hoping to get served. As luck would have it, the bar tender was ex Navy. He told us that as long as we behaved he would serve us.

Three old vets were listening to all this and decided to buy us beers all the way to Los Angeles. One of them was drinking Manhattans, a name I would use many times in California when I would drink at bars underaged from 18 until 21. If I thought there was a chance I might be carded I would order a Manhattan. Not once was I ever carded. I guess they thought if I knew that old man's drink I must be old enough to drink. I'm still fond of Manhattans some sixty plus years thereafter.

Stepping out of the train in Los Angeles was like being in

As I Saw It

Paradise for me. Perhaps Dec 12 just before Christmas was not the ideal time for boot camp but California's palm trees and warm weather looked like a bit of heaven compared to South Dakota.

Our transfer to a San Diego bound train ran us right down where I got my first look at the ocean. There were waves rolling in and I made a comment "wow, there must be a storm out there." Some old guy said "Lad, this will likely be a very long experience for you." Little did I know how true that prediction would prove to be.

Keith Wells

Chapter 3
Navy

It Was San Diego After All

 I must admit that volunteering for boot camp just before Christmas was not my smartest decision but I wasn't finding boot camp as bad as I thought it would be. I had wanted to see San Diego in the worst way for years now. Of course we had now been warned of the jump off the high tower in the swimming pool and the shot in the left nut with a square needle, but tonight on this quiet Christmas Eve it was quite pleasant standing in my shower shoes beside this cement flat sink under a palm tree washing some clothes by hand.

 I looked up through the palm trees and saw this full moon. It was rather nostalgic as I stood there thinking of my friends in Ireton whom I had left behind. Perhaps they were gazing at that same moon at this moment Maybe even my old girl friend Joy was looking at that same moon wondering if she'd made the right decision to bed down this new guy. We were now on opposite shores of the USA. I wondered if I would ever see her again.

 Morning comes early in boot camp with some dummy running a night stick around the variegated inside of a trash can to wake everyone up at zero five thirty. This does not usually put

Keith Wells

you in the best of moods to start the day.

Breakfast passes quickly especially when you are not a morning person and the sight of even good food makes you kind of queazy. By six o'clock we were on the grinder (a huge cement field) ready for inspection. I had been chosen for one of the squad leaders simply because I was tall and could swim. You must be able to swim if you are in the Navy or take lessons every night until you can. My squad had the next to the smallest guys. I was responsible for having them ready for inspection. This included carrying a safety razor in my sock to dry shave any inadequately shaved face. One poor soul got more than one dry shave from me.

The grinder was famous for having seagull poop and people's spit from the colds we all suffered. It was hard to tell which your boot might be sticking to. It was not particularly hot at that time of year but occasionally someone would faint and collapse onto the grinder. Needless to say, that was a mess. None of my squad ever fainted because I warned them not to lock their knees when standing in formation. That caused most of the fainting, not the heat.

In nine weeks we received twenty one vaccinations. No such thing as "I am not going to get a shot" like the covid shot deniers now days. They used huge syringes and just changed the needles for the next guy. One big black lad walked away with the needle sticking in his arm. When I pointed it out to him, he went down like a light.

Firing guns was real shocker for some of the guys but I had been pheasant hunting so many times it was no big shakes. Having to stand in fire gear on a floor flooded with gas while it was lighted up was quite a different matter. I think my crew got that fire out in record time.

Finally the day arrived where we had to jump off the huge

As I Saw It

tower. We were to jump off, rip off our pants to make them into a life preserver, then paddle to the side. It was quite a day just to see everyone in clothes. Usually at the pool we were stark naked. No use having all that extra laundry right?

Well the tower turns out to be no higher than the high board at the Hawarden public pool. Jumping off was no sweat; getting those damned pants off was quite another thing. We all managed to do it tho, even those who had been taking swimming lessons all these weeks. Getting out of boot camp was a real incentive to learn how to swim.

The square needle in the left nut never materialized, thankfully.

Sea The World

When I read the ads that said, "Join The Navy and See The World" I never dreamed it would be through a porthole. I guess I was destined for the Navy. During WWII when I was only four, my much older brother sent me a complete Navy uniform for a child from his Navy base in Hawaii. He sent a lot of gifts like an unpeeled coconut with a painted beach scene, various shells, a harmonica, and toys. These may have been sent to make up for having broken my only metal toy (a wind up bull dozer) by running it off the dining room table. All toys for the rest of the war would be made of wood including a wooden tricycle that I wore a path in the linoleum floor of the dining room floor with.

I'd heard so many stories of the wonders of Hawaii that it never occurred to me that I would not be sent to that island paradise as soon as I finished boot camp. Didn't the Navy send brothers to the same location even if it was fifteen years later? Well ok, a nine month detour in San Francisco for electronics school then on to Hawaii right? What, I have been assigned to a destroyer! Destroyer! What the hell is a destroyer? I would soon

Keith Wells

find out. I guess I should have paid more attention that day in boot camp when we filled out a questionnaire that on one small print line you were asked to select a type of ship you would prefer. A kid beside me said his father had been on a destroyer; ok, what the hell, I'll check destroyer too. What did I care, I was going to shore duty in Hawaii.

Getting to that destroyer named the USS Wedderburn DD 684 was quite an experience in itself. A twenty-two hour bus ride from San Francisco after electronic school convinced me to fly to San Diego after this furlough back home. It was a night flight and sitting by the window looking at blue flames around the engine cowling suggested that maybe twenty-two hours on a bus might be preferable.

When I got out of the cab at Pier 32 I was surprised when I saw how small that ship was with 684 painted on the bow. I was learning sailor speak, "bow." Did you catch that? 369 foot long, 35 foot wide, 30 knots. Not a good match for the some 35 foot waves we would be exposed to soon enough.

The maiden voyage would be what they called a shake down cruise to get us ready for a West Pac cruise, a trip to Japan and beyond. We were sailing to San Francisco where I had just come from. I'd been over the Golden Gate Bridge many times before, but never under it. Quickly I learned that a prediction and old guy made on the train to boot camp when I saw the normal rolling waves of the ocean for the first time and exclaimed "there must be a storm." He said, "this will likely be a very long time for you." My stomach and rolling waves learned to hate each other. If you have never been sea sick, try to imagine the moment just as you know you are going to throw up and extend it for days on end with absolutely no relief. Twenty-one continuous days on one occasion.

Pulling into Pearl Harbor Hawaii was magical. Beautiful

As I Saw It

water, tropical trees, small pleasure boats out in the bay and Diamond Head far up the coastline. It was all I had hoped for; exotic looking people, exotic restaurants, and the famous pink Royal Hawaiian Hotel where we heard Don Ho singing from an outdoor terrace, but of course we couldn't afford the three bucks to get in. The only thing I didn't like about it was in two days we would be leaving and I would not be staying there as I had looked forward to since wearing that tiny sailor suit.

We watched beautiful Hawaii disappear into the horizon as we sailed off to Midway Island. At eighteen, I hadn't learned the significance that island played in the course of the war. But as we sailed into the blue green water surrounding Midway it became abundantly clear that rusting hulks of two sunken ships were not hauled in there for affect. The war had ended only 15 years before and the battered runway and clusters of rusting metal were evidence of a very precarious time in history.

One really astounding feature of Midway was goony birds. Sort of a large, clumsy, overweight version of a seagull. Watch them take off was hilarious. They would try to run down the abandoned battered runway while valiantly flapping wings seemingly too heavy to maneuver, then collapse into a mound of feathers. This could easily take several tries until they would lift off into the most graceful flight imaginable. It was said they could fly for up to two weeks following a single ship for waste food thrown overboard into the sea. It's also rumored that a school of fish died when I left the ship and no longer supplemented their food supply by hanging over the rail seasick once again. I'm not sure how long specific goony birds followed The Wedderburn. One goony bird looked like all the others to me.

Guam was next on our stops. I remember it for suffocating heat, dense jungle terrain, tropical work hours followed by afternoon ship wide swimming time with nets to keep fish away

Keith Wells

from the swim areas. It didn't stop eels though. I came face to face with a four foot long one, which scared the bejesus out of me. Though I never witnessed it, it was claimed that a favorite activity in Guam was bar fights where local Marines enjoyed fighting with sailors who would be leaving soon, thus no retribution. The idea that there were still Japanese soldiers hidden up in the hills of Guam after fifteen years who thought the war was still on was sort of disconcerting.

The main function of our cruise to South East Asia was to sail up and down the Straights of Formosa to protect Formosa and Chiang Kai-shek from the mainland China. We were very welcomed in Formosa.

As we sailed into Kaosiung Formosa (now Taiwan) little kids on rafts would meet us far out into the bay and beg us to throw coins into the sea so they could dive in to retrieve them. At night dumb boats would pull alongside our ship to sell everything from souvenirs to prostitutes. A favorite barter item was the brass casing of a five inch spent shell. Many items of junk jewelry and cigarette lighters could be made from just one casing. One such shell was dropped the catch of which was missed and it went right through the bottom of the flimsy craft. Those artillery guys were something else.

I was quite anxious to get out and sightsee the first chance I had to get off the ship, but it was not to be. The collective opinion was that we were going to the Brown Palace Hotel. We were met by a bevy of very young girls in tight sarongs. Each sailor had his own hostess for your entire stay. You gave her $20 at the door and she kept track of your bar and food purchases throughout the afternoon. My hostess was this cute little 15 year old who I found out had been sent to the Brown Palace to supplement the family's income. I suppose it beat diving for nickels. Long into the afternoon one of the old salts who'd been on cruises before

As I Saw It

said, "take her upstairs, she will do anything you want her to do." Not only was I far too bashful to do that but I felt very sorry for her. Also the films we had seen in bootcamp about venereal disease were fresh in my mind. When she took me out to my petty cab back to the dock she handed me the change from my $20. She was correct within five cents. I tipped her the remainder of the twenty which was about $8.00. She had tears in her eyes. I hoped she remembered me as fondly as I remembered her.

The base of our West Pac cruise was Yokosuka Japan. Most of our refueling and replenishing of supplies was done there. The base was huge and very industrial looking. We rarely got beyond Black Market Alley when going ashore. You had to cross over an open sewage canal that ran sewage to the bay. Lots of bars, restaurants, out door meat markets with indistinguishable hunks of flesh hanging in the open air and street hawkers were there to sell you whatever. A real character was a little old man in black pajamas who was a street hawker for a whore house. His English repertoire was "fucky-sucky?" As we'd pass him he say, "GI what you want anyhow?" When we found out he was a woman, this little fart, Timmy, from the ship would run toward her and say, "You Baby." She would run away saying,"you clazy plik." Normally she'd cross the street if she saw Timmy with us. I never saw any sailor go away with her. I always wondered if it might be a set up for a robbery.

Sasebo was a much more attractive port in Japan where we never spent as much time as I would have liked to. It was very rustic compared to industrial Yokosuka. My favorite bar/restaurant was a wooden structure where you walked along a creek side to a wooden bridge where the entry was. Beer was 25 cents and mixed drinks were 35 cents. A full steak dinner was $1.25. The atmosphere was very laid back and the waitstaff actually seemed to enjoy being there. There was much more of a

Keith Wells

jungle like atmosphere around the city than a bustling city.

One of the very few actual sightseeing tours I got to go on was to Nagasaki where I visited the site of where Fat Man destroyed the city and killed some 70,000 people in an instant just fifteen years prior to my visit. A Buddha statue sits pointing into the air where fifteen hundred feet above, the bomb exploded. It was daunting to be walking around the museum in a US Navy dress uniform among other visitors who you know were affected by that bomb. Most amazing at the museum were six coke bottles fused together from the heat at seven miles from the impact.

Hong Kong was our main stop on the way to Australia; what a glorious city. We were there several days during which I was able to visit a huge outdoor museum of architectural splendor, the floating city of Aberdeen, a beach, and be fitted for a hand made worsted wool suit which cost $21.23. Had I only known the bargains in electronic equipment I would have saved for a year. We were making about $120 a month. Friends were loading up on stereo equipment like Akai tape recorders and amplifiers. Besides the suit I was able two buy my mother a set of china, and myself a camera. My saddest memory of Hong Kong was an old man bent over into a trash can scraping up some discarded food. Life could be brutal in those days. Still is.

Much to my chagrin, Australia was not to be. We had crossed the equator, had our butts paddled, received the crossing certificate and were looking forward to arriving in two days where it was rumored two girls would be there to grab you by the arms and welcome you to Australia. But Captain Wilson got on the mic and said he was sorry but we had orders to return to shell Cambodia. This might have been one of the first conflicts of the Vietnam war. There had to be fifty US ships ten times closer to Cambodia than us. Why our ship? We fired one hundred rounds in the middle of the night to God knows where and then it was back to Yokosuka. Planned stops in Shanghai and the Philippine Islands met similar fates. China closed off Shanghai to all US ships as did the Philippines. No explanation was given to us peons but the US protecting Formosa was a likely cause. Shelling Cambodia didn't help matters either.

Our departure from Japan was cause for a raucous party and and an impending typhoon which is the subject of another short story called Revenge.

Life on Treasure Island

Immediately after boot camp I was sent to Treasure Island off San Francisco for electronics school. This was rather surreal for an eighteen year old from a town in the Midwest of 350 people.

We had views of downtown San Francisco, the Oakland Bay bridge, the Golden Gate Bridge, and Alcatraz. At that time Alcatraz was still operational and we could hear bells tolling dinner and lights out. Since Treasure Island was the closest thing to Alcatraz, it was creepy to have to stand watches at night knowing if anyone escaped it would be to where you were standing watch, alone, at night. We would have to walk by a building down near the waterfront which had hanging hazmat suits that appeared like men standing around, any one of which might be a prisoner from Alcatraz.

Electronics school was ok but would have been easier if I had had more algebra in the famous Ireton High School. I spent a lot of extra hours trying to make up for my lacking math background. Each Friday was test day and each Monday was Blue Monday where we came in to see if we passed or would be dropped out of school which could lead to some really undesirable jobs in the Navy like painting ships. On one occasion I did poorly on a test and had to practically sell my soul to keep in school.

Our free time meant getting on a bus and going over to San

Keith Wells

Francisco. On one of my first trips over, I was walking down Market Street and this guy pulled over and said, "hey sailor, want a blow job?" I was so shocked I said, "WHAT, what did you just say?" And he said, "oh Honey, you just fell off the turnip truck didn't you?" And he sped off!

Luckily for me I had cousins living in San Francisco and Oakland. The San Francisco first cousin was indirectly responsible for my birth.

The Oakland cousin was a custom saddle maker and had a shop on a ranch up in the hills above Oakland. It was great fun to go over and ride horses, often with the little girl my parents had started to raise who was now in her mid twenties. I tried to get this cousin to agree to teach me saddle making, but he was an ornery old bastard and wouldn't do it.

Liberty on the weekends often meant bike rides through Golden Gate Park or a trolley ride to the Buena Vista restaurant turn around where you could walk down to Fisherman's Wharf where my favorite restaurant Fisherman's Grotto #9 was. The whole warehouse area now known as Ghirardelli Square was still just old warehouses. After a great seafood meal, nothing could beat an Irish Coffee at the Buena Vista.

There were two people on Treasure Island that stuck in my memory. One was a beautiful blonde Marine woman who worked in the mess hall. No woman has ever gotten more attention than this poor girl. The other was this short-bus character that ran around the base with his hands held up like on handle bars of a bike as he muttered putt, putt, putt. He was imagining himself on a motor scooter. Rumor had it that when he got his medical discharge for mental reasons he putt, putted up to the gate and just walked off. The gate guard said, "hey, what about your motor scooter?" His reply was "you can have it. It got me where I wanted to go."

As I Saw It

As I was packing my sea bag to go to San Diego to board the USS Wedderburn DD684 I was thinking why couldn't I have thought of a motor scooter!

My First Cruise To San Francisco

When I got out of the cab at Pier 2 in San Diego, there she sat. This huge number 684 painted on the hull. The USS Wedderburn really didn't look all that big; not at all what I expected. Later I would find out it is in a class of one of the three smallest ocean going vessels. 369 ft long, 39 ft wide. A typical aircraft carrier is over 1000 ft long.

As I was shown what would be the sleeping quarters, I was amazed that 18 people could sleep in a space the size of a modest living room. Bunks were stacked three high. I, being junior, would be given a top bunk which was ok except for the fifty cables about a foot and a half above my shoulder. This sleeping compartment was the furthest point at the bow of the ship; thus maximum bounce and constant sound of water hitting the metal just beyond your face.

The next person to arrive after me was Andy who made a grand entrance by coming down the ladder backwards. We knew this would be interesting. Two other guys, Ray and Al made up my new click. Al said he was from Burnt Corn, AL and Ray was from Lodi, CA. We never quite figured out exactly where Andy came from, but numerous alien places were suspected.

My electronics shack was as far from our quarters as structurally possible which I approved of since I was always anxious to get outside but you weren't supposed to be outside during working hours without a reason for being there. So it worked well for me except on occasions where the sea became so rough that we had to move back and forth on the third deck while clinging to lifelines attached three foot inside the outer rail.

Keith Wells

The first couple of weeks were pretty good. We worked with an older fellow named Robby, who was married and in his mid twenties. He instructed us on getting ourselves familiar with the location of all the radio equipment we would be working on henceforth. Robby would be getting discharged after a major cruise we were preparing for which was called West Pac, i.e. western pacific cruise. This cruise was looked forward to by most everyone. We'd first be stopping in Hawaii, then Midway Island, Guam, Formosa (now Taiwan), Sasebo & Yokosuka Japan, Singapore, Hong Kong and Sydney. I'd wanted to visit Hawaii and Sidney for years and couldn't wait to get underway. Singapore and Sydney would never come to be.

Before this endeavor there was much preparation for what they were calling a shakedown cruise to San Francisco. I had just come from San Francisco where I was in electronics school so it was no big shakes for me. It would be interesting to pass under The Golden Gate Bridge instead of going over it. I had driven and walked over it many times.

The big day came and with great fanfare as we and our two sister ships pulled out of the harbor. All was well and incredibly beautiful but then we hit what would become my nemesis, the breakwater. Suddenly the ship started this side to side sway and a gentle but distinctive bounce. Now some of the old salts began to mumble about how San Diego to San Francisco was always a rough ride.

Very quickly my stomach started doing flip flops and soon I was on the rail feeding the fish. I was not the only one not enjoying their first taste of the sea (which tasted a lot like breakfast) since I observed that several of the other nubbies were a similar shade of green.

This condition was not made any better when this little dick named Timmy arrived. When he found someone who was

As I Saw It

obviously not too well he would let out this barfing sound and drop his pile of plastic, but very realistic, puke right on the table in front of them. Always the victim would grab his tray and run for a trash can. Timmy also loved to come up to a sea sick prone guy at breakwater and sing, NOW IT BEGINS, DAY AFTER DAY. Or he'd delight in telling you he'd just had great green gobs of greasy gopher guts for lunch. All round nice guy.

When the ship finally arrived at San Francisco I didn't even feel like going ashore. A week or so later when we arrived back at Pier 2 in San Diego as I was walking down the street going into downtown I felt as tho I was still bouncing and swaying like we were still at sea. I remember thinking screw this I am going to Mexico and learning Spanish.

A Trip to the To The Top

The South China Sea is famous for typhoons, but this is ridiculous. It is one thing to sit at your work bench and be tossed around by waves that can reach 35 foot high, but this was getting serious. How many times in the early days of this WestPac cruise had I sat on top of the desk on a cardboard box eating crackers and sipping water so I would have something to throw up besides green stomach bile. Thank God I had finally learned to control the dreaded sea sickness. It doesn't help to find out forty years later that the Navy gives medical discharges for anyone suffering this malady. But in 1960 my condition was described as "wussy."

Just then I was paged to the bridge. That almost never happens. Something was wrong, very wrong. If a radio was down, word got to me by way of your Junior Officer in Charge, Ensign Black. Damn, I would swear he was 13 tho I was only 19. How did this pint sized twerp get in charge of three men! He did not respond well one time when I reported the problem with a radio connection to the bridge watch as O.O.T. (Obvious

Keith Wells

Operator Trouble)

When I arrived at the bridge Captain Wilson was there. Oh boy! Something isn't right. I haven't seen him as concerned since the day I was called to the bridge only to find Ensign Black on the floor in a pile of puke. He'd lost radio contact with the aircraft carrier, our flagship.

Captain Wilson quickly explained to me during the torrents of rain smashing the windshield of the bridge that a line on the mast that allowed reception of radio signals had broken in the wind. So we had lost contact with the flagship. He also mentioned that "someone" would have to go up there a hundred feet plus off the main deck to fix it in the midst of a smaller than usual but never the less daunting South China Sea typhoon. Andy, the other electronic technician had already informed me, and the world, that they could shoot him. He would NOT go up on the mast. I'd been up there before for maintenance but never at sea.

I was comforted by being told that the first boiler had been shut down so that if I happened to fall I wouldn't fall into a red hot smoke stack. I'd fall a hundred feet into a cooler smoke stack! I was so relieved to hear it.

As I began the assent, I felt a tap on my shoulder. I saw this huge braid of gold on his cap. Captain Wilson said "you be careful up there son." With two linesman belts on and tools including a soldering gun attached to the belts, I slowly made my way up the ladder to the first platform. From there, there is a pole with a precarious ladder attached that while taking 30 degree rolls and bouncing about 25 feet you attach one belt to one rung, then attach the second belt to the next rung, finally reaching the top. Now I have to say it is hard to achieve success when a lot of the crew are watching and cheering fall, fall, fall! Should I have fallen we would have had to return to port to retrieve my battered, semi cooked body from stack one.

As I Saw It

The intricacies of how to solder a line to a connection in pouring rain and swaying and bouncing on top of a pole a hundred and fity feet off the water is very different from the working down on the main deck and therefore hard to describe. Suffice it to say, I jerry-rigged a wire to hold the radio line to the connector. Then shielded the spot to be soldered from the driving rain, plugged in the soldering iron, and soldered away. Thank God I had by this time learned to control sea sickness for there was little time for that.

When I got down, some of my better friends were cheering and the Captain said, "nice work son." I was quite relieved to hear they had tried radio contact with the flagship and my repair had worked. From that day forward Captain Wilson spoke to me on the very rare occasions he would see me. I was devastated when he was replaced by a Captain who was a real dork and would allow only classical music to be played on our onboard radio system.

Revenge

The day ended like many others onboard the USS Wedderburn while on duty in the Pacific Fleet. We were in port at Yokosuka, Japan expecting to leave port tomorrow for the return to the U.S.A. The ship had rented a bar in town to throw a raucous party. Two thirds of the crew could go and I was among them. I had however heard from one of my radioman friends that a storm was brewing, so I sold my spot to another guy who really wanted to attend. Late that afternoon I walked out of the radio shack and glanced over my shoulder; what I saw in those rather ominous clouds and that stifling humidity struck a fear chord in me brought on by days at sea battling sea sickness.

While all of those lucky bastards at the ship's party were eating and drinking, the remaining third of us onboard began

Keith Wells

preparing to go to sea. The Captain and Quarter-master were keeping a close eye on the storm. We expected to leave the next day.

By midnight the party crew were called back to the ship early. Since a storm can move a 369 foot ship around enough to damage it and the dock, the Navy wisely(?) goes to sea in even the worst of typhoons. What the hell were they thinking!

Before one a.m. all of the crew who had been on liberty were back. Of course they were piling in bed being very drunk from the party. All hands of the third of the crew who had not gone to the party were on deck to prepare to cast off as soon as all the crew were gathered. As I watched the drunken bunch file in, I anticipated what was going to be another gut wrenching experience at sea during which it was not uncommon to take 35 degree roles and bounce 30 foot high. Waves hitting the windshield of the bridge on the third deck were not uncommon.

Once we hit the breakwater the fun began. We had learned early on that you hold onto everything. In the mess hall during meals one hand firmly holds your metal (divided spaces) tray so that it or its contents didn't go flying off the table. We electronics guys put all the tools away in special containers that would keep them safe. Coffee cups were gripped with a deadly grip lest your favorite souvenir cup should go crashing to a metal deck. Radar men actually held buckets between their legs so they could watch the rotating screen and barf without missing a beat. For me, tracing schematic diagrams of radio equipment in stiflingly hot little rooms while bouncing and rolling often left me running to the rails.

As usual, I felt that feeling you get just before you know you are about to throw up. I had learned over the months to control the sea sickness although you never feel good when in a storm at sea. I remembered when eight "friends" in my division would

As I Saw It

harass me about being sick a lot. We were now well into it. Those who got the ship underway that were not sick, found breakfast not to be very appetizing. It seems our ace Samoan cook, whom Timmy called Blow-face, was among those not feeling well this morning. He was up and around and amenable to a proposal I had for him. I had a couple of crackers from the mess hall that I asked "Blow-face" to spread a generous bit of his prized limburger cheese upon. He became as giddy as I when I explained the plan.

I went back to our very cramped 20' X 30' sleeping area which sleeps eighteen men. It was not quite daybreak and none of the party goers were up yet. I quietly placed our 30 gallon corrugated trash can in the middle of the floor. I then went to each of the eight out of sixteen who had taunted me at one time or another, stuffed the limburger delight under their noses telling them "since you missed breakfast, I brought you a snack." Then I jumped back as they sprung out of bed and barfed in my strategically place garbage can. All but one old salt, who had been around a long time, jumped up and threw up including the devil's disciple Timmy. I had never felt better about being at sea.

Epilogue:

Several years after this event I used this story as an oral presentation for my first college speech class. The instructor gave us two minutes to come up with "a speech that would make him remember us forever." When I finished I looked back at him. His glasses were pulled up on his forehead. Tears were running down his face and he was wiping them with a handkerchief. He called me up after class and told me he had been a Navy Commander. Needless to say, I got an A plus.

Austin Healey Sprite

On one of my leaves from the Navy I went to visit my mother at my grandparents home in Springfield, MO. My grand parents

Keith Wells

were then in their 90's.

My Uncle Charlie had married a woman who owned an old fashioned diner with a long row of only counter seats all topped in dark red vinyl. I liked Uncle Charlie despite my father saying "he was worthless as tits on a boar." His wife was very pleasant to me and my mother, but she crossed a line with me that was unforgivable.

Some poor older (at least older to me at the time) black gentleman came to the rear door to order some takeout. I was sitting right beside where he came in. She said "you know I can't serve you Jim." The sad look on his face will be etched in my mind forever.

I went across the street to the car dealership where old Jim worked to apologize, but he was not there. On the way out, I see it. Powder blue. Classic bug eyed English design. An 1961 Austin Healey Sprite. It was love at first sight. I went back and convinced my mom that this was the car for me.

I took my father's 1950 Ford back to the dealer and negotiated a trade which my mother co-signed as this would be my first step at credit.

I could not have been more proud of a vehicle. To me it was an Aston Martin. I'd be leaving in two days to return to San Diego to finish out my enlistment. I packed up the little jewel and away I went. It was rather unheard of to stop for the night to rest in those early days of being twenty something. Driving straight through was the general gist of things.

Well about 20 hours later that routine lost a lot of favor. I woke up just as my bumper was easing under the rear of a semi truck. When my eyes popped open, all I could see was trailer doors. I was so shocked I don't think my eyes closed all the rest of the way to San Diego.

Driving that little gem around San Diego and Los Angeles

As I Saw It

I felt I had reached the top. Twenty one years old, an E-5 in the Navy, and driving a brand new sports car.

Ship In Dry Dock

When a ship comes off an extended West Pac cruise it is customary to put it into dry dock for painting and repairs. Like our sister ships, we headed for Long Beach Naval Shipyards after a couple of weeks of R&R where wives and girlfriends rejoined their significant others after six months of separation.

Going into dry dock is like going into a lock that you would see on a river except all the water is drained out and the ship is left standing on blocks. Being in electronics, I was not a part of the painting crew, and since all radio equipment was shut down there really wasn't a lot to do but spruce up our shop and tools.

The first week end I took a bus down to San Diego to pick up my little blue sports car. We would be there three months so having a car was a real advantage. Early on, the car needed an oil change so I started scouting out neighborhoods that had a service station close to a restaurant/bar. I found one that advertised oil change specials on their marquee and low and behold a bar-b-cue restaurant right across the street.

There were two entrances so I selected the restaurant side and sat at a long counter with stools. I told the sort of middle aged waiter I wanted a bar-b-cued pork sandwich. Before I could order a drink he said, "a draught beer with that?" I tried hard to act causal and said "sure that sounds good." He did a refill with just a nod. As I left he said, "drop around tomorrow night, we have live music."

I selected one of my older looking underaged buddies and we went back that next evening. It was a quiet, laid back neighborhood joint with really good food. Of course Navy food was not a really high bar to surpass.

Keith Wells

As time went on we would add more and more friends and it wasn't limited to Fridays. On any given night there would be as many as ten guys from the ship. On music nights maybe twenty since some of the local girls heard there would be dance partners available.

The waiter who first served me turned out to be the owner and we became quite friendly. He knew me by name by this time. He'd say, "hey Wells, good to see you." When the end of our stay came he put on a special party for over twenty of us. It wasn't free, but it was a two for one night before such a thing was common. We had a great time and hated to see our time in Long Beach end.

I called him aside and thanked him for all the good times we had. I also said, "you know most of us are under 21." He said, "yes, but I couldn't afford not to have you guys! I have made as much in three months as I usually make all year."

The Purple Onion

North Beach was about halfway between downtown San Francisco and Fisherman's Wharf. This was the hot, live entertainment center where you could find all kinds of cooky people all hours of the day and night. This was the gay community before The Castro district was even thought of, and a real tourist trap. My cousin introduced me to this area.

North Beach had a New Orleans style bar playing jazz until late at night. For a draw, they had a very sexy lady sitting on a stool at the back of the bar. Curious gentlemen would peak into the swinging doors, see her sitting there, and stroll on in to check her out. Only problem was, she was a mannequin! Most of these tourists were too embarrassed to turn around and walk out so they would buy a drink.

One evening after several beers, one of my Navy buddies

As I Saw It

and I came upon what appeared to be a strip club. It was called Finocchio's. Each gal that came out to sing or dance seemed better looking than the last. Our favorite was this slim blonde with great legs and nice boobs!

We were clapping and whistling our heads off when this black lady about 35 beside us said, "you do know these are men don't you?" Men? Really? With boobs and all? Well she told us Finocchio's was a female impersonator bar. We were most embarrassed.

When the show ended all the "girls" came on stage and removed their wigs, even the blonde with great legs and boobs. The lead singer introduced the black lady beside us as a jazz performer at The Purple Onion, a great small music bar there in North Beach. With that she acknowledged the applause and left.

We sat through the next set just to re-evaluate the performance and try to see how we could have been so duped. When we closed out the show, I found The Purple Onion singer's keys on the floor. I picked them up and walked over to The Purple Onion, but it was already closed.

Next evening I went over early to The Purple Onion and asked if I could speak to her. She recognized me and said, "oh honey, did you find my keys?" She comped me a front row seat and bought me a couple of drinks for her show. She said if I would stick around 'till the end of her last set she would properly thank me. Being only eighteen, I wasn't sure what she meant but I slipped out of there as soon as she started her next set.

Woman Love

Gene Vincent had a recording out called Woman Love. His rendition on stage was very controversial since he gyrated around kind of like Elvis who was in a lot of trouble for doing just that.

Well that was reason enough to compel six of us at the Naval

Keith Wells

Base in San Francisco to rent a station wagon and drive down to Hayward to see him. The local police had warned that if he sang that song they would raid the club and arrest him. What a draw! The joint was packed.

All through the concert everyone held their breath thinking the next song would surely be Woman Love. But not until the last song did the familiar refrain come blasting through. About halfway thru the song, true to word, a police whistle blew and they were coming through the door.

For most of us, this WAS our first rodeo, but we had been smart enough to sit right by an exit and out we went. Being naive and cheap, several of the guys grabbed their cans of beer and high tailed it for the car thinking we'd really outfoxed the police. We couldn't hang around to see what was going to happen to Gene since only the guy who rented the car was old enough to be in the bar.

We were not two blocks away and a police car was on our tail with lights flashing. Panic! Not only were we drinking beer underage but doing it in a moving vehicle!

There was only one cop who stopped us and he was a very serious middle aged, no nonsense guy. He shinned a flashlight in the car. One of the panicked front seat guys had stuffed his beer can into the glove box and beer was running out of it.

The cop said, "oh Christ, you jerks are from the base aren't you?" We kinda nodded a yes, and he said, "are ANY of you of age?" The driver nodded a yes and was reaching for his billfold.

The cop says, "you get the hell out of this town, and don't ever come back!" I took his advice and I have not been back to this day.

Coffee House in San Diego

When I arrived in San Diego in my new Austin Healey Sprite

As I Saw It

I was on top of the world. I'd be getting out of the Navy next year on a six month early out to attend Chico State University. Little did I know that day would never come.

Days off were spent cruising up and down Highway 1 enjoying the sunshine with the top down. After a trip to Tijuana to buy a tonneau cover, I rarely put the top up unless it was a hard rain. My saddest moment in that car was having a motor cycle cop stop me for having three people in a two seat car. As he was writing a ticket he put his big nasty boot up on my fender to have a knee to write on. I was livid, but he and I both knew a Navy boy would never challenge a cop.

Since my shipmates were frequently out to sea, I had a lot of free evenings alone. I was now attached to the hospital where I had a job while I wore a cast on my arm. Bars weren't very good entertainment since I was not into drinking alone. So I sought out coffee houses.

The early 60's brought a lot of Kingston Trio type folk music which really caught on before the Beatles arrived. I'd gotten to see the Kingston Trio live in San Diego so I was pretty hep on that sound. It wasn't long before I discovered the best way to hear live folk music was at coffee houses.

One of the more interesting coffee houses I found was out on El Cajon Blvd near San Diego State College. My hair was allowed to be a little longer now that I wasn't on the ship, so I didn't stick out like a sore thumb. Arriving in a new sports car didn't hurt either.

I thought I was kind of transitioning from service life to college life. When I would start a conversation with some of the college kids I found out two things quickly. I was at least three years older than they were and they weren't quite convinced I was ready for college friend material.

I did meet one interesting character there though. He

Keith Wells

had been in the service too and was an artist. He drew comic characters like Beatle Bailey in the newspapers, but he was way ahead of the times. He had enrolled at San Diego State and had quickly seen the girl of his dreams.

He tried a most unusual approach. As she was walking along he would speed up and turn directly in front of her and say, "can I interest you in me?" This went on for a while and she finally became amused or just gave up and they started dating. They were going to be married at the time of my last contact with him.

To say this coffee house was laid back would be an understatement. It looked more like someone's poorly decorated living room. Most of the seating was old upholstered, overstuffed chairs and couches. Along the far wall was a long narrow bar with wood stools. You had to turn your stool away from the bar to see the stage.

I loved listening to the very casual musicians playing their rendition of folk music. But most of all I loved sipping my newly found coffee treat cappuccino. Had I not developed a lactose intolerance I would still probably be hooked on it today.

Tijuana Taxi

In our last year of Navy service, Ray Riesling (yes, just like the wine) and I shared a studio apartment on W. Point Loma Blvd in San Diego.

Our tiny refrigerator was stuffed with XX beer. (Dos Equis) Johnny's Mission Beach pub was just a short drive over the bridge from Ocean Beach to Mission Beach. The usual Friday night treat was a two block walk up W. Point Loma Blvd to Consuela's Mexican Restaurant. Her enchiladas were to die for. I will always remember Ray digging out a carrot from a jar on our table during our first visit. Little did he know it was marinating in jalapeño sauce. Never had seen anyone down a whole XX in one swallow!

As I Saw It

Ray turned out to be less than discretionary in many instances. He lit our gas oven after leaving the gas on to find matches. It blew him across our tiny kitchen into the cabinets across the aisle. He had very limited vision, or was it discretion, after two beers. He would drag home these beasts of burden that he picked up where ever and proudly bring them home. Kind of like a cat would drag in a dead mouse.

Ray didn't have the finest pallet as well. No matter what the fare, it must be smothered in ketchup. One of our less stellar visits was a popular Italian restaurant in downtown San Diego. We both ordered the spaghetti meatball special. Ray had already had his first beer so his judgement was in question already. No sooner had we been served than Ray asked for the ketchup bottle to drowned the spaghetti sauce. The chef promptly threw us both out with a warning to never return. In Ray's defense I must say that almost all the food on our ship needed considerable amounts of ketchup.

Ray and I decided one afternoon that we really should experience Tijuana, so we took my car to the border and walked across. It was early afternoon so we found a pub that served food. Well actually it was a strip club that served food. Halfway through lunch the show began. Being early in the day it was beginner's try out time. This very young but very cute girl was trying what I would assume was her first try at stripping. I personally thought she was doing fine, but of course Ray having had the second beer was ready for the professional girls. He started chanting put it on, put it on! Again we were thrown out of a restaurant/bar.

Having had several more beers, we now decided to head back toward the border. About a block away we came upon a guy with a donkey cart. The cart had a sign saying "Tijuana Taxi." It was not a taxi at all but a place to get your picture taken on a donkey cart. Ray was up on the seat in a flash. With Ray's ten word Spanish

Keith Wells

vocabulary a verbal battle ensued about the requested payment.

In turning about to follow the proprietor's movement, Ray somehow kicked the donkey who turn his head and tore Ray's shoe off. At this moment I panicked and said "come on Ray we're heading for the border. It was only two blocks but quite a sight nevertheless. I was running like mad leading the pack, closely followed by Ray with one shoe missing, the donkey owner and a Mexican policeman. As we approached the gate into the USA a woman border guard saw me reaching for my ID. She just waved at me and said "keep on running." I never have been in Tijuana since. You can't be too careful.

Balboa

Have you ever asked yourself what might have been different if I just hadn't done that one little insignificant thing. One such thing for me was stepping off a moving "cattle car." (A low truck trailer used the move people around the Naval Base in San Diego)

I was chatting with a guy and saw that we're pulling away from my stop. I said good bye and quickly stepped off. My feet hit the ground but I bounced up and tried to cushion the blow of falling on my butt. My right hand bent way too far over, but I thought I would be ok. A year later when I had applied and been accepted to attend Chico State College on an early out, I was at a doctor's office for a cough when I was asked if there was anything else that was bothering me. I mentioned the wrist, and was promptly whisked off to X-ray the wrist. Low and behold I had a broken navicular in the wrist. No wonder that wrist hurt when I was using screwdrivers in my electronic repair job.

Since the whole right arm to the elbow including the thumb was now in a cast, I was sent to Balboa Naval Hospital in San Diego. Little did I know how life would change. I was assigned a job as an assistant to the head of orthopedic surgery. Besides keeping the office straight and cleaning our shared bathroom, my most important function was to line up the Commander's X-Ray's for each patient coming in on a given day. This was quite routine except for those days when a younger female dependent was scheduled. I guess everyone but me knew there was a clear outline of the patient's breasts on each chest X-ray. Go Figure!

There was this one particularly attractive, five years younger than me, dependent with particularly nice outlines. I would talk to her, Lynn, when she came in and watch her slight limp as she walked away. Seems a horse had thrown her and she caught her foot in the stirrup so she was dragged a ways. Thus the limp. It did give her butt a most wonderful twist as she walked away. I wanted to ask her out so badly but my access to patient records revealed that she was a Marine Corps Captain's daughter. Marines and Navy are like mixing oil and water, so I was quite sure her father wouldn't approve.

Finally one day I gathered the courage to ask Lynn out. Her reply was "my god I thought you would never ask." We did the usual San Diego dating thing; San Diego Zoo, a coffee house near San Diego State, walks along La Jolla Beach and various restaurants all over the beach area. Soon I was asked to dinner at the family home. She had a brother a bit older than her who apparently was quite into this girl friend. Lynn's mother began calling me herself to ask me to dinner, "and by the way could you pick up a bottle of Vodka at the commissary?" I thought she really liked me. Little did I know she was a flaming alcoholic and was asking me so I would bring her a bottle of vodka each time.

Our most memorable dinner was one where Lynn's brother was missing. Half way through dinner they got a call from Paul. He and the girlfriend had run away to Vegas to get married. Seems he was further into her than anyone knew since she was pregnant. What an inopportune day to have picked to ask her

Keith Wells

parents if I could take Lynn to Navy Day at Disneyland. Long and short of it, I did get permission to take her to Disneyland which was a good hour plus from their house.

Navy Day was a roaring success. The Navy had rented Disneyland for a whole day. Any sailor in uniform could attend and ride all the rides for free. When we left late in the evening one of the west coast's famous fogs rolled on in. We could literally see two car lengths ahead for fifty miles. We were three hours late and met by very anxious parents. "Why didn't you just stop and get a room?" I looked that beady eyed Captain in the eye and said "you don't really think I am that stupid do you?" He soften up to me somewhat, but when he and his wife would go bowling he would reappear claiming to have left his bowling bag. He couldn't really think I was that stupid could he? He often tried to get me to go albacore diving with him. Alone, out on a boat, under water. I guess he really did think I was that stupid.

I had several friends from the ship I had been on before transferring to Balboa: Ray, Al and Andy. Ray and I had a studio apartment in Ocean Beach. Andy and Al had an apartment near the zoo. Ray, Al and I used to love to drink Andy's prized Cutty Sark scotch and replace it with cheap crap. Of course he couldn't tell the difference despite his claims of only Cutty was worth drinking.

Well old Al from Alabama had a friend who loved to drive around and drink beer. One unfortunate night we had 15 beers. I have no recollection of driving the 15 miles to downtown but I was awakened by a street sweeper going by my open car window at 6:30 a.m. in downtown San Diego. After returning to Balboa I parked the car on the street instead of employee parking because it was closer. By 8:30 I was having chest pain that was severe so I went to tell the Commander. By noon I was unconscious for three days and had been to surgery to sew my right eye shut

As I Saw It

because it had been swelling so much. Apparently they had had a staph infected person admitted who gave it to eight people. One died, I was the next most serious.

When I awoke and saw my mother there, I knew I was in deep doo-doo. She never had seen an airplane much less been in one. The Red Cross had flown her out saying I had very little time left. Many antibiotics were pumped into me but Vancomycin, an experimental drug which I was told had been previously used to cure infections in cows tits, saved my life. None the less I was in quarantine for five weeks. One year to the day in Balboa, six months in a cast, and six months fighting staphylococcus aureus infection of the lungs and right eye, all for having stepped off a truck.

Several days after Mom had left, Lynn appeared at my bedside. I remembered my car was still on the street. Apparently she'd stopped by to see me and got the keys to move my car into employee parking. Lynn faded out of the picture and went back to dating high school boys. Turns out she was only 17. She had claimed to be 19. I was 23. No wonder her dad was trying to trap me. I guess he thought I knew, but I didn't.

On the five weeks of quarantine this particular night nurse kept coming into my room without a mask. I warned her, "you do not want what I have." When I was finally out of quarantine I asked her to dinner at one of my favorite beach restaurants. We dated several times but I knew an officer (Lieutenant) and an eleven year younger, non commissioned officer had no future. I left for home without saying goodbye. She wrote me a letter saying she would never trust a man again. How many people were hurt, myself near death, from one stupid mishap off a truck? Not to mention Chico State was not to occur. I wonder how it would have been different. Water under the bridge as they say.

Keith Wells

Ocean Beach is Now Dog Beach

About six months before I was to be discharged from the Navy I was assigned to Balboa Hospital in SanDiego because I had a cast on my right wrist up to the elbow and you couldn't go to sea with a cast. Like I could swim hundreds of miles anyhow should the ship go down.

Not wanting to sleep on the ward with actual sick folk, I got an apartment in Ocean Beach just two blocks from the water on W. Point Loma Blvd. My roommate, Ray, was still attached to the ship, so frequently I had the whole place to myself. By whole I mean one large room with a couch and a Murphy bed that pulled out of the wall. We would rotate nights on the bed while the other slept on the pullout couch.

Side by side behind the living room was a tiny kitchen and a tiny bath. Outside the kitchen door was a little sitting area where we kept a bar-b-cue. By crossing the back of the property we had a straight shot at the convenience store with easy access to beer and cigarettes. I didn't really need the cigarettes but Ray smoked. I had been drinking beer illegally in bars for four years and that convenience store was the only place I was ever carded. Not for beer mind you, but for buying Ray's cigarettes!

Down W. Point Loma Blvd. opposite the ocean was Consuelo's Mexica restaurant. They were known for the best enchiladas in Ocean Beach. My favorite memory of the place was the first time Ray and I went in for dinner. There was a jar of carrots, beans and peppers sitting on the table. Ray, thinking these were hors d'oeuvres, fished out a carrot and popped it into his mouth. It had been soaking in pure Jalapeño juice and ol' Ray downed a beer trying to put out the fire.

Mission Beach across the canal north had a great boardwalk for biking along watching bikini clad girls sun bathing. Frequently

As I Saw It

they gathered in groups to watch muscle bound men working out with weights on the beach. One day I was riding a rented bike along the boardwalk (which was actually cement) when I almost ran over an older lady while I was watching one of these gatherings. She wasn't particularly mad, she just said, "I wish you young bucks would be more careful." I tried to be thereafter.

There was one house way up the beach that was particularly famous. Not so much for the huge bay windows that overlooked the beach, but for its notorious tenant. Seems this guy got a thrill out of guys barreling oranges at his bare butt. I never witnessed this perversion, but it made a great conversation piece around town.

Another famous resident of Mission Beach was this gorgeous, very flirty blonde. Everyone I knew tried to get a date with her, but tho very much a pal with all the guys, she would only date black boys. This was NOT common, and not well taken, in the early 60's. When questioned about it, her reply was, "they will spend every dime they have on me and they are hung like a horse."

There was a special little bar in downtown Mission Beach called Johnny's Surf Club. This was the absolute epitome of an early 1960's surfer bar. It had open areas where huge windows should have been, a stand up bar, several old tables that fit the era, loud music, and keg beer. What a place. If you visualize a surfer bar in your mind, this was it. I loved that bar. I still wear their green ball cap with the blue visor.

On a visit 44 years later I found my apartment on W. Pt. Loma Blvd to look exactly as it did in 1962, even the same color of paint and trim. However, our beloved Ocean Beach was now called Dog Beach! I don't even like dogs! What the Hay!

Keith Wells

Chapter 4
Chicago

A Visit to Chicago

After my release from Balboa Naval Hospital in 1963 I was torn about whether to seek employment in electronics or finally get to college after my delay for having been in the hospital for a year. Six months with a broken wrist and six months with a hospital staph infection. Either way it would be back to California.

Since I was sent home to await my discharge I decided to visit three guys who were from Ireton, now working for American Airlines in Chicago. I thought it was ironic that it was me who took an airline correspondence course to work in the airlines but three buddies were the ones took jobs there.

One of my earliest memories of the visit was when I came back to the apartment complex of rows and rows of fourplexes. I went into the apartment where one of my friends was staying and there was a girl sitting there reading a magazine. I said hello and headed into the bathroom. When I returned I asked her if she was a friend of one of my friends living there. She said "no." I said "well who are you?" She said "I was about to ask you the same thing. This is my apartment." I had the wrong look alike duplex!

Keith Wells

I found out that a huge employer in Seattle had recently laid off two thousand electronic technicians so I decided to give a bank teller job a try. My first post Navy job would be with Citizens Bank in Park Ridge. I was introduced to a tall red head named Rick who had also been in the Navy. Rick taught me the fine art of rolling bags and bags of loose coin that vendor customers had dropped off for deposit. We would roll thousands of dollars worth of coin a day and would occasionally find we were off by a few cents. Rather than go through all those rolls of coin we had an over and under bag hidden under all the loose bags. If we were over we'd drop a coin or two into the bag. If we were short we'd raid the bag. Since the coin machines were set very tight we would occasionally be over enough to get a six pack after work, tho Rick was never much of a drinker.

Rick's primary interest was music as he was a professional drummer. I once got a chance to see Santana's Sergio Mendez and his three year old kid play Congo drums in Rick's basement. Rick would take me to places all over Chicago that would eventually lead to an introduction to my first wife. He often played at the Playboy Club. A shame I didn't get to go there. In return for all this entertainment, I provided him with aspirin for his frequent headaches which his Scientology parents would have no part of.

Early on Rick introduced me to The Pic a restaurant directly across from the bank. The Pic served a rather nondescript type of food that you might find in a department store restaurant. Not outstanding but far above Navy food.

I had an apartment I shared with a guy named Jones which was right down the street within walking distance of the bank. Jones could go days without saying one word. One Sunday evening Rick showed up to pick me up for dinner at The Pic. I asked Jones if he wanted to join us. He said "where ya goin'?" Rick immediately pipes up with "Jones, Jones, Jones. That's all

As I Saw It

you ever do is talk." Poor Jones didn't know whether to shit or go blind. Although Jones wasn't much for company, I loved sitting in the living room with my feet up on the heat register sipping beer and watching all the traffic on North Western Avenue as the snow fell on the huge lawn.

Citizens bank was a constant source of entertainment. I was later made a teller both on the line and in outdoor pop ups which were literally elevators that popped out of the ground in the parking lot. Occasionally someone would not see that one of the pop ups was now up and they would back right into it. There were several memorable characters working the pop ups besides me. One old guy smoked Wings cigarettes all day and you could hear his cough echoing across the parking lot. Another couple, Bennie and Karen, were the epitome of a Chicago couple.

Bernie met Karen at a hair dressing school where he enrolled to meet women. He always claimed they were going to start a salon called Bernie's Coiffeurs With Snatch To Match. Bernie was going to do the snatches while Karen did hair. Karen was unfortunately killed when a woman putting on makeup ran over her bike. Saddest funeral I have ever attended.

Rick talked two old guys into taking karate. One was an old guy, probably fifty, who needed exercise. The other was a restaurant owner who was always getting robbed. This fellow worked only on a powerful side kick and put several would be robbers in the hospital.

There was a pretty, petite girl at the bank named Sally that I dated a few times. On our first date I took her to a night club on Mannheim Road near the airport. Unfortunately Rusty Warren was the comedian and chose Sally as her victim. First thing she said when we sat down was "my god honey, that's the third guy you have been in here with tonight." Poor Sally. We did have one last date where she asked me if I would be willing to raise our

Keith Wells

kids Catholic. I told her I was just hoping for a nice quiet dinner, I didn't know we were going to start a family.

After Jones moved to Phoenix, I got a room in a house. The old German couple left me while they traveled frequently. So I pretty much had the run of the house. They had a slobbery boxer named Bo Bo who would invariably stuff his slobbery face right in my crotch as I was leaving the house. I hated that mutt, but at least he didn't bite like Rick's nasty dog named Skipper. Rick came over to this house one evening for his aspirin fix. He was really in a stew. Seems his girlfriend had called and broken up with him. Rick said "I answered the phone and she said, Rick we are through. Goodbye." Hello, hello!

I wonder how much of this stuff ol' Rick remembers? I remember it all like it happened yesterday.

Carol's Family

It wasn't too long after meeting Carol that I was invited to dinner. The first time in their narrow Chicago cold water flat, Carol's mother, Ruth, decided to make chocolate malts. I heard all this commotion going on out in the kitchen. When I strolled out there to see what was going on, there was iced cream, milk, and chocolate all over the kitchen. The two of them were laughing their heads off. Ruth was embarrassed but I could tell then that she had a great sense of humor.

Carol's father, Pete, was an Electrolux vacuum cleaner salesman. I had never heard of Electrolux, nor met anyone like Pete. On my first dinner with the family he asked if I wanted a beer. This was not a custom I was used to but I said sure. He set down a full quart of Meister Brau in front of me, the old widowed aunt Ann and himself. I wasn't prepared for this custom but I was in the Navy so I was accustomed to beer.

Pete took me to his local hangout bar right in the center of

As I Saw It

Germantown. He seemed to enjoy introducing me as a Navy vet. I guess this legitimized me or his daughter's selection. I'm not sure which. Pete's drink of choice was a boiler maker. A shot of whiskey with a beer chaser. I heard after he passed away that his only complaint of me was that I didn't drink enough. I have certainly made up for that fault.

Carol's older brother John was a musician; a tuba player. He played in a polka band, played at some Chicago Bears games and taught music at a far south side all black school. Many of his students came from poor black families so John owned about half of the jazz band instruments they played. John would lead that group of kids to the state champion jazz band finals. He rewarded kids with camping trips all over, even Colorado where we were living.

Her younger brother, Budd, (actually Peter Jr.) was quite athletic and became a coach. But at 14 when I met him he was accident prone. He hit his head coming down off a diving board, cut his bicep badly with a chain saw and got beaten up. Some guy had gotten lost and stopped Budd to ask where he was. Budd told him, "Chicago," and he got a beating for the wise guy remark.

When I decided to take six months off on my early retirement trip, I got lectures from all the immediate family including Budd. Having been on my own since 18, I was quite unaccustomed to taking unsolicited advice from anyone especially a teenager. But Budd and I would become great friends later on. We developed a special gay handshake that would crack us up and roll many an eye.

Aunt Ann was a special lady and I liked her very much. She was an avid Chicago Cubs fan and watched them all the time on a little black and white tv in the kitchen. I truly loved her cooking but I later wished she had spent more time teaching Carol to cook. But that kitchen was Ann's domain. Not even Carol's

Keith Wells

mother told her what to do in the kitchen.

Aunt Ann gave me a tie for Christmas one year. It was dark blue with cut outs for pink balloons with yellow strings hanging down as if they were floating in air. Carol and I called it the Sperm Tie because it looked like several sperm swimming upstream.

Bless old Aunt Ann. When the lectures started from the family about my proposed six month early retirement trip at 30 years old she said, "you just go ahead, do what you want and have fun. There will come a day when you will be glad you did." I did, and I was.

To sum it up, Carol's family was great to me, and great for me.

How About You, You Want a Piece of Me?

Meeting my buddy Rick in Chicago was a social bullseye. I would never have found some of the many Chicago haunts, that only the natives knew about, without him.

Maxwell Street Market was a prime example. I would never have even driven though that area much less get out to shop for whatever Rick was looking for on that given day. His story of having an entire engine stolen out of a Corvette he had parked for 45 minutes was all I needed to convince me that I really didn't need anything from the flea market.

Mooney's Bar was another locals hangout. It was a short order bar specializing in hamburgers and Chicago's local beer called Meister Brau. I loved the time of year when Meister Brau served dark beer. Chicagoans told me that was when once a year they cleaned out the vats and dark beer resulted in using the sludge. I'm hoping that was a joke. Mooney's most memorable feature was white parachutes hanging all over the ceilings.

Rick would drag me along to gigs where he was playing drums in the band. Sometimes I would entertain myself by dancing with the wives of other band members. Both of us benefited. One of

As I Saw It

his more memorable acts was down near Rush Street which at the time was made famous by such entertainers as Dick Gregory. Well Rick and I were hot footing down Rush Street and this limo pulled right in front of us at a crossing. Rick simply opened the door, slid across and went out the other door. I did not follow.

One week end Rick took me to a Thanksgiving turkey shoot. The better shotgun shooters could win a turkey. But this was not shooting clay pigeons like in skeet shooting. No, no, these were live pigeons released on the ground from covered mechanical release traps. It was dark in there so often the pigeons were blinded by the bright sunlight. A couple of these "sportsmen" actually shot at them while they were still on the ground. We took offense to that and were cheering the pigeons who managed to escape. We were politely asked to leave.

One evening Rick talked me into going to a dance at the Congress Hotel in downtown Chicago near Lake Michigan. Rick saw a college friend Kathy who introduced me to Carol Weber whom I would later marry. At the end of the dance after pleasantries and phone numbers were exchanged Rick and I were headed to the elevators where a loud drunk was verbally abusing everyone. I got into battle-ready by getting Rick between me and the guy. This loudmouth said to Rick, "how about you pussy, you want a piece of me?" Apparently Rick did because he hit this guy so quickly and so hard in the stomach that he threw up on the spot. Rick said "come on, we must get out of here quickly." Be careful of whom you ask "do you want a piece of me."

Keith Wells

Chapter 5
Boulder

Indian Peaks Burial Ground

Hiking was a biggie in Boulder in the mid 60's to mid 70's. Eleven mile hikes were a week end norm. My God, we have climbed Long's Peak together! It couldn't be that trekking up to Diamond Lake in Indian Peaks was that big of a deal. But Mike was dragging today.

We were sitting on this huge boulder and I was explaining that this pulmonary surgeon in Balboa Hospital had told me I would never live beyond 35 without this massive lung scraping operation. I'd been told by a patient who had it done six months ago, "just die, it will be much easier." That was enough to convince me, but it has been ten years and I have to have a plan in case that cussed doctor was right. Mike was an integral part of this funeral plan. The ashes would be carried up by my best friend and spread out among the flowers in front of Diamond Lake where I had stopped to reflect on the beauty of this spot dozens of times.

Mike was protesting now, "why me? You have a son. Let him do it." "He is only going to be one year old when I hit thirty-five," I reasoned. He was not convinced I was dying for it was him who was panting and gasping for air not me. This was going to be a

Keith Wells

hard sell I could see.

It was rather strange how we connected, Mike and I. He was actually a year younger and into his first few years of teaching at UC Boulder. I was just out of the Navy about four years when we met. I was a junior then. Now I was out of the undergrad program and working at First National Bank of Denver. We were able to get together more often now because there was not the teacher/student stigma, though I had never taken one of his classes. Everyone knew we were friends and I didn't want to embarrass him by having to deal with me in class, plus I didn't want to chance doing poorly in his class and embarrass myself.

We had helped each other a lot over the several years. I'd helped him move; he'd helped me install a fireplace. We often had lunch together somewhere on The Hill in Boulder or down on Pearl Street. It would be Mike who later would direct me into college teaching.

Occasionally I was invited to parties at Mike's place where other faculty members were in attendance. No one ever asked why I was there. I guess by now everyone knew we were friends. I wore a beard in those days; red it was from that bit of Irish kin I had. At one of those parties, Mike's wife grabbed me by both sides of the beard and kind of shook my face. She said, " I have always wanted to do that!" Being undaunted by that, was I gently cupped her halter top clad boobs one in each hand and said, "I have always wanted to do this." She screamed "MICHAEL!"

Copious quantities of beer were responsible for such actions on my part, but I actually was brought up with respect for women. My mother would have died a second death had she witnessed that act. I was quite prepared for some serious consequences especially in the company of several of Mike's teaching buddies but what happened instead as they all laughed. One came up to me later and said, "God, I have always wanted to do that."

As I Saw It

Well even this close camaraderie was not going to convince Mike to trek up Indian Peaks with my ashes. Not then nor during the rest of the years I lived in Boulder. As for my son, when he was much older I pointed out Indian Peaks from down below and his response was more or less forget it. I guess I am destined to spend eternity in a brass bottle.

From Boulder To Richmond

The drive in a 26 foot Ryder rental truck from Boulder and a dry 78 degrees to Richmond with 98 degrees and 97 percent humidity was quite enough of a shock. But when I arrived at J. Sargent Reynold'sCommunity College and found out school would be delayed two weeks to complete the construction of the building I was REALLY shocked. I was definitely wondering if I made a mistake passing up a job offered late at Arapaho Community College in high dry Denver. Why didn't that offer come in before I accepted in Richmond?

We had a first day faculty meeting, me in a tan corduroy sport coat with western boots and nearly everyone else in three piece suits. I figured I may as well let these southerners know they had a westerner on board. My attention was drawn to this rather skinny black fellow in a shiny maroon, three button suit with a cream colored, frilly shirt and patented leather maroon shoes. This lad was making a statement as was I.

First thing Dr. Bowers told us about school being delayed and we wouldn't have offices for a month or more. Then he asked if anyone had any experience with electricity. I raised my hand and said that I did have some experience in the service. He said, "do you think you could install overhead lights?" I said yes, then he asked if anyone would volunteer to help me. Jerry, my soon to be new black friend in the bright suit volunteered. We got to know each other's off beat humor very quickly as we installed

Keith Wells

class room lights.

The office situation was chaotic. Eight of us were crammed into a room with four desks on each side. Jerry and I took the last two on the left. As the weeks went by, Jerry and I tested the limits of our joking around. We had students coming in to just listen to our banter. Dr. Bowers quickly decided I would be given the very first private office that became available just to separate us.

"Foreigners" like me were not well received by true Richmonders. Several of us misfits like Jerry, a fellow from a downstate Virginia tobacco farm, a black law prof, a pretty blonde from New Jersey who had attended William & Mary, an outcast heir to a nationally known publishing company, an Orthodox Priest who taught English, a black woman named Florence from NC, and a fellow destined for a doctoral program in Oklahoma next year formed a group friends. I never heard that any of us was ever invited into a Richmonder's home.

After a brief stay in a third story apartment, we bought a home which had a view of a shopping center parking lot. I quickly erected a board fence about halfway down the back yard to block this pristine view. Not bad after that, our side of the shopping center was far too far for most people to walk so not much traffic.

Jerry helped me move in and I saw people peering through the blinds at us. When we finished, I slapped Jerry on the back and said, "I think you're going to love it here!" He said, "oh Jesus, you are going to get me killed!"

One in our group was a very memorable character. The publishing company heir was given a generous amount of money per year to stay way, so he had a stately home on Monument Ave in Richmond, and threw a Easter party there one year for all the outcasts. He had an old aunt visiting who was having a birthday.

Monument Avenue was closed off for the annual Easter parade. It was quite hot, so our host went across the street to offer

As I Saw It

a band a place under his tree IF they would turn around every hour and play Happy Birthday to the aunt. They were pleased to do so and the senile old aunt thought this whole parade with throngs of people dressed in antebellum costumes, pushing huge wheeled baby buggies up and down Monument Avenue was put on for her birthday.

I found quite a few students at JSRCC to be first in their family and ill prepared for college level accounting course work. I spent a great deal of time teaching basic math, especially fractions and decimals. One poor soul needed one more accounting course to graduate and came to me with his plea. I had first encountered him in the year before in Accounting 101. We had a word problem with a question that entailed the cost of a Christmas wreath. I'd called on this lad to read the problem and give us a solution. He stopped reading at the word wreath. He had never seen that word and had no idea what it meant.

When that final exam occurred this student was very worried. I saw him pacing back and forth in front of my office while I was grading papers. I finished his and found out he had passed with a D, but he had disappeared from the hallway. I walked down to a railing that overlooked the student coffee shop. One of my teaching friends, the Orthodox Priest, was standing by the rail and I was explaining the situation to him about this kid.

Just then the kid saw me and I gave him a thumbs up. He let out a war hoop and came running up the stairs to me. I told him he made it with a D and he was so excited he picked me up off the floor, danced around in a circle and sat me down. The Priest, being a very calm sort said, "what do your students do if you give them a C?"

Keith Wells

Chapter 6
Okoboji

22 Orchard Lane

It became obvious that teaching at an all Catholic college may have been a mistake. After an over zealous president of the college near Chicago where I taught had decided that granting tenure was not going to happen any more, a bunch of us who had dutifully done all the requirements decided this was a dead end. It would now be year to year contracts like a part-timer or one who couldn't meet the requirements of tenure. We bailed out of that school like rats off a sinking ship.

My next selection was a four year college which seemed at the time a natural progression since I would be moving up from a community college. This would be the first time I'd taught the classic Accounting wipeout course, Intermediate. Many a fledgling prospective Accounting major met their own personal Waterloo in Intermediate. I was generally forgiven for scheduling an exam on a religious holiday, but it seems having a few beers in downtown Madison and actually dancing with some of my women students was verboden. One staid old nun asked me next day "Exactly how does one boogie when fraternizing with our female students?"

Keith Wells

I knew my days were numbered when I mentioned to the Dean, another nun, that I was afraid my department chair, yet another nun, was becoming senile. Invariably she would ask me to a meeting and forget she told me, or not ask me and swear she did. Apparently one does not criticize nuns at a Catholic school no matter how incapacitated they may become.

A little community college in Estherville, Iowa would become my next career stop. We had two days to look over the school and the area. I met my prospective office mates Dave and Ron. Little did I know we would also soon become neighbors. Dave set me up with a local realtor named Ken. Ken was as a master salesman. He routed our visitation through some of the shittiest properties in Estherville, then climaxed it with this gorgeous house on a beautiful cul-de-sac which was priced well below the property prices we were used to around Chicago. We loved it, but told Ken that we would have to sell our previous home first.

Ken and his lovely wife took us to dinner at a restaurant overlooking Lake Okoboji, which I had visited as a kid many times before. What a salesman that old Ken was. He had us sold on the house, the town, and the neighborhood before dinner had ended. He had even arranged a financing plan to expedite the sale. When we moved in some few weeks later, moving into 22 Orchard Lane was like going to fun camp. Ken had hand picked us to be his across the street neighbors. Ron lived across the street as well and Dave lived around the corner.

I had expected to hire some locals to unload the U-Haul truck the next day but here came the whole neighborhood to help unload. Ken, his next door neighbor and I were moving this heavy refrigerator up a short stairway. I was insisting that it would be much easier to rent an appliance dolly the next day. But the neighbor, an ex cop, insisted "Oh no, no use wastin' ten bucks." That error in judgement cost me a knee surgery and 40

As I Saw It

years of pain because the two of them released their grip for a second and the full weight of that refrigerator came down on my left knee.

I didn't realize the knee damage at the time, so a raucous beer party on our back deck with pizza from Woodie's would follow the move in. Living on Orchard Lane was such fun. Every night was a potential beer party at one of the neighbors' houses. Weekends often meant a twelve mile ride over to The Lake for drinks at Tweeter's, the bar in the Emporium, or Rueben's pub.

The exact same amusement park called Arnold's Park sat where it did when I was a kid. It had one of the only existing wood roller coasters still in existence. Dave was very much involved in starting the Okoboji Rock and Roll Hall of Fame. Often some well known musicians would be playing at Arnold's Park.

Life was always entertaining around Orchard Lane. When I built a small tool barn down on the slope behind the house, I would find all the neighborhood kids waiting patiently for me to begin work each morning. My daughter's free spirited propensity to strip naked and run around the cul-de-sac always drew a good crowd. She was only three then and has ceased that activity at 44 I believe.

We went down to the local grocery store the first day after arriving. I asked for the manager to see if I could write an out of town check since we hadn't set up a local bank account as of yet. He said "are you new in town?" I said "yes, I will be teaching business subjects at ILCC." "Oh," he said, "you must be Mr. Wells, you won't need cash here, just give the clerk your name and we'll bill you monthly." Then he personally carried our order to the car. That would be anonymity in small town U.S.A.

I was under care for debilitating migraines for most of the time we lived in that house on Orchard Lane. This was diagnosed by my doctor who it seems had owned our house before us. I was

Keith Wells

put on Inderal and could only drink Coor's Light beer because any other alcoholic drink would trigger a migraine. It wasn't until I moved to Albuquerque and the migraines disappeared that I found out they were caused by an allergic reaction to a hemlock tree growing in the back yard.

It was very rare that anything happened in the cul-de-sac that everyone didn't know about. We hired one of the cutest girls in Estherville to babysit Scott and Susan. She had a habit of laying out on our back deck to suntan while the kids napped every day. Our neighbor painted one side of his house three times so he could watch her. Also, if you were missing for too long over your normal routine, questions would be asked. I snuck out of our neighborhood with only my usual Levis and white tee shirt on to drive to Omaha for an interview with the University of New Mexico.

I was soon found out when no one saw me the next day. A neighbor asked Susan where I was, and when she said "Omaha" it was a dead giveaway that I was on an interview trip somewhere. No one would go to Omaha during the week for anything except a farm related trip or to catch a plane. Since I had nothing to do with agriculture and I was traveling alone I had to be going somewhere on an interview trip.

There would be much explaining to do when I got home. The interview trip was primarily to visit old friends who lived in Albuquerque not that I had a chance at a four year University accounting position. That required a doctorate which I had unwisely let slip away because my jackass doctoral department head asked my opinion of what I thought of the program at Virginia Tech. Had I just known all he was asking for was an ass kissing I would have puckered up. He didn't have to black ball me for telling the truth!

Little did I know this big cowboy with the shinny boots and

As I Saw It

silver tips on his cowboy shirt was the Dean and would offer me a 26% raise and an entry into university level employment. When I got back to Estherville I had this monumental decision to make. Stay at ILCC or take a mammoth career jump. There would be hell to pay. My name would be mud from my wife, my kids, the neighbors, the church and the college. It was a decision to advance my career that to this day I question whether I made the right decision.

Horner's Stories

While living in Estherville near Lake Okoboji, Iowa I met an interesting character named Horner. He actually loaned me the down payment for our house so we could move in across the street from him. Being a realtor, he sort of hand picked his neighbors. Some of you readers who think I can spin a tall tale should have met Horner.

He had two stories that never failed to get a rousing response every time he told them around the old beer drinking crowd - despite his wife Jean's groans at the thought of hearing them again.

One concerned his having received a bow and arrow for a birthday in his youth on the farm which I THINK was in south eastern South Dakota. His parents warned him time and again about using chickens as targets. This particular day was no different as they got into the car to drive into town and left Horner alone at the farm.

Well Horner had a field day chasing chickens, and along about the time the parents were due back he shot an arrow at a chicken and it actually pierced the reddish wattle under the chicken's throat. The wattle was acting like a fulcrum supporting this see-saw arrow and chase him as he might, Horner couldn't catch the poor thing to retrieve the arrow.

Keith Wells

Just then his parents pull in and ask him if everything had gone well in their absence. Horner assured them that all was well just as this chicken came running out of hiding with an arrow in its wattle.

Another of Horner's stories involved shoveling snow off his roof. Up in the mid-west it wasn't uncommon to see people push snow off a slight inclined roof to relieve the weight of a heavy snow. On one particularly heavy snow, Horner was on the roof and decided to shovel the snow more or less into one pile so his young son Kelly could play on a snow mountain.

When he completed the task he thought he would just step off the roof onto the pile rather than go down the ladder he had come up on. He stepped off but sank like a rock, hands over head, into snow so far over his head he couldn't move. When he looked up all he could see was blue sky. All he could do was to shout out at young Kelly, who thought this was a game. Horner finally convince him to go fetch his mother who once again had to dig him out of trouble.

These two bonus stories are provided buy my buddy Dave Peterson.

At one time, Horner was selling medical equipment to hospitals. The company held a sales meeting in the winter at a ski resort. The meeting was at one building and then lunch was at a second building that they were to walk to, maybe 150 feet away. Their path took them across the top of the ski run and Horner got a little too close to the slope and with his leather shoes with leather soles, he started to slide sideways down the ski slope. Thinking that he had no other choice, Horner jumped at a 90 degree angle so his shoes were pointing straight down the ski slope, just like a pair of skis. Horner couldn't stop himself, and he took off skiing down the slope using his leather shoes for skis. About halfway down, a little kid riding up the chairlift, yelled to his dad, "Look, Dad - that guy's skiing without skis." Needless to day, Horner was a big hit at the luncheon.

Another Hornerism. The Horners lived in a split level house, with four different levels. When walking out of the kitchen, there was a set of about six steps that went down to the family room. Immediately beside that set of stairs, to the left, was a set of about six steps leading up to the master bedroom. One night, Horner (perhaps after consuming a "Horner Special" or two), turned off the kitchen light, so the house was dark. He proceeded to the stairs leading up to the bedroom and leaped up to the second step. Only problem was, Horner was too far to the right and when he jumped up, he actually was at the six steps leading down to the family room.He flew down the steps into the family room and he banged himself pretty good, including a finger that ended up at a right angle to the other fingers. A visit to the doctor was required.

The Poets Club

I really hadn't been at Iowa Lakes Community College all that long but I was happy to be away from the craziness of the small Catholic college I had suffered through for one year. I had gotten to meet several of my fellow teachers, all of which made a lasting impression.

Dave was a couple of offices down from me. To me he looked like Rod Stewart the singer. He was an aspiring author and would write incessantly between classes. Our Dean of Business was a character named Harry whom we called Harry the Magnificent. Harry was very busy seeking legitimacy. He'd enrolled in a Doctoral on-line, rubber stamp program and so wanted to be referred to as Doctor. All he really accomplished was driving between the three campuses of ILCC daily to "check on people."

A rather unique agreement was struck between Dave and

Keith Wells

Harry. Dave would do Harry's class scheduling each semester if Harry would leave him alone on his daily check ups. Harry was only to happy to comply since he regularly screwed the schedule up and booked two or more classes in the same room at the same time every semester.

Ron, who had an office next to me, and I found out lived across the street from me, was a CPA that had his sights on starting his own CPA business in town. Ron had great hopes for me joining his practice, but teaching was my forte not hovering over tax returns.

Ed was an English and Speech instructor. I have used his first story told to me many times. Apparently he'd given an assignment for students to bring in a demonstration. One of his students brought in a very small, obviously sick live pig. The student was going to show how this pig was dying of a type of lung ailment that affected pigs in confined quarters. He hooked alligator clips on the pig's nose and tail then plugged in the electric cord to which the clips were attached. This promptly electrocuted the pig. If that was not dramatic enough, he then began cutting the little fellow up to show the class its damaged lungs. Ed was not doing so well himself but half the class had run for the bathroom.

Early on, Dave had given me a nickname that has held to this day in some circles. The Doctor, or Doc. I didn't have a real doctorate because of a little misunderstanding with my doctoral degree chairman at Virginia Tech so this could not be construed as a legitimate title, but it was not the first time I had been called Doc. I was Doc the talkative dwarf in the senior high school class play of Snow White when I was six years old and in first grade.

I always wondered why Dave called me Doc. I suspected it was to frost poor old Harry's shorts because he wanted to be called Doctor, but it could have been the beard which could have been construed (like it was in Richmond, Virginia) as the mad

As I Saw It

Doctor. It may even have been just because the student cafeteria served a drink that tasted like Doctor Pepper but was called Dr. Wells.

Keith Wells

Chapter 7
Albuquerque

It Shouldn't Happen To A Dog

His name was Phil. I don't know why that struck me as odd. The Veterans Administration hospital in Albuquerque had a lot of unusual names; my god Albuquerque is pretty unusual when you consider it has three times used the letter "u." Phil was head of urology at the VA. I was in my forties. Little did I know that men of my age would soon be asked to drop trou, stoop over, and take a deep breath.

Phil was missing one day and his questionably abled assistant was on hand to snap on the dreaded blue glove. I'm not sure but either said questionable assistant was trying to kill snakes while up there or he was just naturally sadistic. Either way the next day I was peeing blood. Now penises are used for several reasons but passing blood is not a preferred response.

I was forced to call Phil to report this revolting development and to caution him that I was NEVER to see his assistant again. I was a Veteran for Christ's sake! Phil said to come in tomorrow. He would have to examine my bladder because blood in the urine could mean a cancer issue in the bladder. I didn't really have to ask Phil what the exact route to the bladder was because I kinda

Keith Wells

knew. Phil assured me it was a quick and "relatively" painless procedure. He did not explain relative to what.

Next day I thought about the procedure all through morning coffee and decided I really didn't want a solid round tubular flashlight stuck up my poor little dingy which by this time had shrunk to childlike dimensions. So I had some more coffee and a chocolate doughnut. Along about 3:00 p.m. Phil calls and says "did you forget something today." I said "no Phil, I didn't forget, I don't want to do this." I'd had experience with military doctors suggesting treatments that really weren't necessary. I'd heard of one instance an orthopedic surgeon who wanted to chop off a leg because he was a fledgling prosthetic practitioner. Well nevertheless Phil convinced me to come in for the procedure.

I was very pessimistic about the whole event. Even when two (not one, but two) younger nurses were sent in to prep me. One of them was holding little Willie up by his foreskin while the other was painting him with an iodine colored liquid. All this time one of them is telling the other about a date she'd had. Needless to say, little Willie was at an all time record low extension.

Finally Phil comes in. I could barely stand to look at this instrument of torture but I had to see it. In those days it was a solid tube about eighteen inches long with sort of a bulbous end. First Phil took a common ketchup bottle of something and squirted into said target. Knowing how squirrelly I had become Phil kept asking, "you ok?" I wouldn't say it was comfortable but so far so good. Then he gets pensive and says "this is going to hurt a bit. Take a deep breathe." What does he mean hurt a bit; he never mentioned hurt a bit before.

When the instrument started in it was at a 45 degree angle to my line of sight, but now Phil pushed this thing down parallel to my legs and shoved it through the prostate into the bladder. That part really hurt. We're not talking child birth but it's up there with

As I Saw It

root canal. All the sudden the bladder starts filling up with water. It was by comparison almost pleasant to the point I thought I was going to pee all over the place.

Soon thereafter Phil removed the thing which went out much easier than in. Phil says "you're all done. Are you ok?" I said "it was great for me Phil, how was it for you?" The two nurses went into a giggling fit and ran out of the room. As it turned out, it was, as a lot of previous military medical experiences, unnecessary. Everything was fine. It was that this assistant was just unnecessarily rough.

That first pee was urinary bliss. The deadening fluid he had put in with the ketchup bottle prevented any pain. I'd never had a longer or more contented pee. The very next time was quite a different matter. I causally took hold of a towel rack in our tiny bathroom and when that stream started it burned like wildfire. It surprised me so much I ripped the towel rack off the wall.

Epilogue

For those of you men who are who are approaching that age, the procedure has improved considerably. You'll still get one nurse with an antiseptic wipe, no iodine painting, a flexible camera tube, and no push down or jamming it in.

The First Time Is The Hardest

The first divorce is by far the worst. I agonized for years over that first divorce. The first inkling of panic might have been on my wedding day. My buddy Rick and I were riding around in his car and I was in a complete twit. Rick said "Well hell, just don't do it if you are not sure." A hundred and fifty guests are invited, my mother and several family members had driven miles and miles for this blessed event. A church would be full of people three hours from now. A banquet hall was reserved and paid for by her parents. There was no way I could back out now.

Keith Wells

It is ironic that Barbara, a very dear friend of mine, would relate the exact story of how if only one person would have encouraged her to NOT go through with the marriage, she would have jumped on the opportunity regardless of the thousands of dollars her parents had laid out to have her marry a complete asshole. She cried the entire route from Santa Fe to Los Angles where they were honeymooning. The marriage lasted exactly one year.

Despite my panic attack, the wedding went off without a hitch. A hundred fifty well boozed guests. A newlywed's dance was great. (I'd had many dance lessons during my bored days in the Navy in San Diego four years prior). The father daughter dance went off with only a few tears from her poor father. Thirty two years later I would find out what that dance was like for a father of the bride.

My second inkling of a mistake would be on the honeymoon at the Playboy Club in Jamaica when a bunny posed with me for a picture. I looked at that perfect specimen of womanhood and realized all my wild oats had not been entirely sowed.

We did well together tho, Carol and I, for six years. She was more or less amenable to anything I wanted to do including taking a six month retirement trip at thirty years old. It was on that trip when I became keenly aware that Norwegian girls had a special attraction to me. Two young Norwegian girls in a train station particularly caught my eye. Neither likely would pee on the best part of me but I now felt the seven year itch a year early. I would later find out how disastrous that attraction the blond Norwegians might be.

On that European trip I confessed my desolation of our union and suggested we re-examine our future together upon our return to USA. Upon return however, the normal routine over ran any discussion of the impending disaster we had discussed in

As I Saw It

Copenhagen. Shortly thereafter I was convinced by her that we needed children to complete the marriage.

One day an announcement came "I'm late!" I was actually elated. A child! Something I never dreamed would happen to me. Her pregnancy was quite easy and Scott was a little joy. Two years later I was advised by her that a second child was a must. Having grown up as an only child, tho I had siblings old enough to be my parents, I didn't fully understand the concept. But her reproductive urge was burning hot.

The second child was much more difficult. Considerable sickness, a near miscarriage, and a baby girl born as blue as the sky. We were scared to death, but the doctor gave her a whack on the butt and she let the world know this would be a voice to be reckoned with. There was never a question of which child in the nursery was Susan; she would be the loudest one. Having two great kids made the marriage worthwhile.

The beginning of a two year separation was preceded by a cross country move, leaving old friends, a job that was threatened by one University Department trying to dissolve another and Carol's newly found love of a new church constantly worked on my mind. Her love of the church superseded all other interests. A counselor later told her this was a substitute for a working marriage. I told her once that I could not compete with Jesus.

Getting my own apartment was not difficult. But the afternoon I had to take the kids, six and ten, into my arms and tell them I loved them but I was going to live somewhere else for a while was heartbreaking. Sunsets were the hardest for me. I was bombarded with guilt at leaving the kids.

We fell into a routine of shuttling kids, trading kids every other weekend and it soon became the norm. Barbara, the same friend who didn't want to marry her first, and now girlfriend of a guy living near my apartment, suggested counseling and

Keith Wells

to go back to Carol after two years and give it a try if I was so undecided.

Marriage counseling only proved something I had suspected for years. She confessed to the marriage counselor that she did not marry me for love. I had some suspicion of that all along. She said "after a time I thought I would learn to love you." That was small consolation when I felt I was about fifth down on the list of people and things she cared for. She wanted security and kids and had that. I guess we were to coast on into retirement from here on.

I did try a last ditch effort by inviting her to a picnic at a park where I told her I was thinking I should move back into the house for us to give it another go. I asked her what she thought might change if I did. Her answer was "Well I wouldn't need a baby sitter any more." Wrong answer! I filled the divorce papers immediately after lunch.

The second wife was as different from the first as night and day. I somehow thought all women were as calm and non opinionated as Carol. Oh my God, was I wrong! I suppose the difference was the initial draw for me to Deb. We had a lot of fun in the nine years we were together, but my impending forced retirement would become a serious issue. The University's Business School had been trying for thirteen years to dissolve the General College which was a community college within the university. The business part of that program grew like wildfire and this was a threat serious enough to get 33 of us fired, rehired in other departments, or forced out of UNM. In my case it was a buyout.

Deb had fairly recently gotten a Bachelor degree in Santa Fe and now was a hot commodity in the accounting field which was scrambling for employees, especially women employees. So my plan of traveling after my buyout became more and more in jeopardy. I had taken a one year teaching job in Guadalajara and we were walking on a beach in Melaque, Mexico when she says to me, "I think you should go on with your retirement plan - alone."

I tried to hold the marriage together by agreeing to have her work a couple of years while I waited. This turned into "I want to work, maybe five years", which turned into "I am applying for full time career employment at UNM." My old school of all places! A work friend of hers suggested she would be much better off with her group of friends than being stuck with an old retiree. Shortly thereafter I would be in an apartment again and another wife would own a house. I would leave Albuquerque soon thereafter and start a whole new life by joining two separate singles clubs in Tucson.

It was much easier this time; kinda like riding a bicycle.

A Friend In Need

Things had been going down hill for months with Carol and I. Church now engaged Carol's time for three or four days/nights per week. Each time I was baby sitter, of course, regardless of the course prep time I needed to prepare given that I was now teaching in a university not just a community college.

The day came when the split happened. I had to gather both kids and tell them that I loved them regardless of the tumultuous period we were about to experience. I had an apartment about half a mile away. When I left the house to check into it and returned for my things, they were laying in a pile on the garage floor. All my clothes, a card table with two chairs, a box of camping dishes and cookware, a couch we were giving away, and all my personal effects, books and all.

A few trips in my trusty Ford pickup had all the stuff in my new digs except the couch. An offer of a six pack of beer was enough to get a passing kid to help get the couch inside.

Keith Wells

My very first weekend took me to the apartment pool with my Sunday newspaper. Some slightly overweight but very friendly woman said "my god, you look like shit. Would you like to join our group for drinks and dinner?"

This was my first exposure to a singles group, many of whom were recently divorced, who treated this whole experience like returning to a college campus. Every night was party night at someone's apartment, and always some accommodating person would make a communal dinner. Tho the upheaval of separation often paralyzed me, this blessed woman who initiated me into an instant social group was a life saver.

I was forty four at this time and quite unprepared for an invitation for a date at El Patio Mexican Grill by an incredibly beautiful twenty four year old who chose two triangles of white cloth to cover two voluptuous breasts for our first and last date. I was brimming with pride just to walk her into the restaurant. Little did I know this whole invitation was to make jealous her boyfriend who was co-owner of the restaurant. Much to my credit, it must have worked. He later apologized profusely for his misdeeds and yielded to the pressure of an aging college professor to mend his ways.

Thankfully for me, a new friend's girlfriend befriended me and started bringing cooking utensils, recipes, and accessories to supplement the meager box of camping gear I was left with. This person, Barbara, would become a very close friend for the rest of her life. She would die of lung cancer caused by secondary smoke from her ex husband. I don't believe either of my children liked her despite her efforts to befriend them. RIP Barb.

During this period of time I befriended another friend of a friend who owned a decorating shop. Artificial flowers, gifts, etc. He gained the name Bill the Flower Fluffer. When others found reason to abandon him when he came out, I found it a privilege to have his friendship, and do until this day.

When divorce finally consumed our marriage I felt I was blessed to have made so many friends who accepted me and what was occurring in my life without judgement.

Dan From PWP

Dan was the first guy I met at PWP (Parents Without Partners) after separating from Carol. Dan had two kids about five years younger than my two. We all had kids, that was what this group was all about. We all had kids and we were all alone; either divorced or had had a spouse die.

Although we were years apart, Dan and I had a lot in common. We both had two kids, a boy older and a girl younger. We like country dancing, pretty women, fishing, cars and beer; especially beer.

We arranged it so that we had our kids on the same weekend. A favorite pastime was to take all four kids to this cheap pizza parlor that had all kinds of games for kids. We'd feed the kids pizza, buy a strip of game tickets for each kid, buy a couple pitchers of draught beer, then sit back and watch all the young ladies who were there for the same reason.

Dan gave me a lot of his time until he hooked up with some woman. Then she would have his complete attention until they would have a blow up, then he would be back at my door. One such affair was a single woman who lived across the street from his house. She was wild as a deer and would do unmentionable things not suited for this story.

Another girl whom Dan had met at Ruby's country bar seemed to me to be ideally suited for him. She had a kid and a home up in a little town in the mountains. She was very level headed, not flighty nor flirty and seemed quite smitten by Dan. Dan was so smitten with her he sold his house to move in with

Keith Wells

her.

One night rather late in the evening there was a knock on my duplex door. It was a Dan and he was in a real huff. Apparently the girl had kicked him out of her house and having sold his house he had nowhere to go. After much hand wringing about getting back in her graces, he gave up and moved in with me. We had bunk beds and a full bed in each bedroom so there was room for his kids when we both had them on alternate weekends. It helped that Scott was old enough now to help baby sit the others.

There was a short lived marriage and new house for Dan until he came home and found a man's leather jacket on the couch. Seems the new wife had an old boyfriend she was still fond of sleeping with. Dan came over and said she told him he should leave the house and he would likely lose it in a divorce. I told him to get back there right now and kick her ass out. She had no rights to his house, so he did, and kept the house.

Dan's third marriage turned out to be a friend of the girlfriend in the mountains who had kicked him out. She was exceptionally cautious in their relationship, but eventually agreed to marry him and they are still happily married. Persistence pays.

Ruby's Country Bar

One of the hot spots for Albuquerqueans was Ruby's Bar on the east side of town. There was a long waiting hall to stand inside while waiting to get in since the city would only let so many people in at a time. Everyone was carded.

When you got in, there was a long bar against the right side wall, a band across from the bar, table seating at either end and a stand up rail bar around the huge dance floor complete with a brass foot rail. This stand up bar was referred to as the Corral since men, and sometimes women, would stand around it trying to make eye contact with a certain dancer whom they might want

As I Saw It

a dance. Since the normal pattern of country dancing is to travel around the floor in a circle, should a woman make direct eye contact with you a couple of rounds in a row, she was interested. Sort of a pre-Match.com.

On one particular evening when I was getting dressed to head down to Ruby's, Sue, my daughter, hands me a black and white pair of nut hugger briefs saying "here, wear your lucky underwear!" I guess she was ready for someone in my life too.

I was sitting at the bar when more of an acquaintance than a friend sidled up and asked me to join him at a table. Seems he had serious hots for one of the two girls at the table; I was to be a decoy for the other.

When I approached the table this head of long black hair turned to greet me with a smile and piercing black eyes. I was definitely interested and hadn't even made it to the Corral. When I asked her to dance, I realized this little troll was under five foot tall. Four foot eleven she would claim.

I learned she wore a size 00 Levis which were nearly impossible to find so she shopped for Levis in the little boys stores. No one in Ruby's, male or female, would wear anything but Levis. Also cowboy boots and hats were a must tho I am sure most of them had never been on a horse. I had, but I don't know that it gave me any particular advantage in country dancing.

Well I did date this particular small person and found out that being in a relationship with her was like being on a roller coaster. The peaks of highs and the depths of lows. We learned our birthdays were the exact same day but 10 years apart. Don't know what that meant except if mood swings were cyclical our road down that cycle was perilous..

This little troll hated kids and it didn't help that I had two, and in summers I had them 24/7. The kids came to call her The Wicked Witch. I don't believe that she mistreated them; she just ignored them. This was particularly hard on Sue who was used to everyone paying lots of attention to her.

On off summer months I had the kids every other weekend. The kids mother, Carol, had a habit of charging into my apartment to pick up or drop off kids. She wanted this divorced ritual over as quickly as possible. Well on one particular morning she charged into my duplex and there sat the Wicked Witch cross legged on the couch in her 00 Levis doing her nails. She looked about thirteen years old. Never again did Carol charge into my house unannounced without at least by a knock.

The Wicked Witch had what she called PMS. Post Menstrual Syndrome. She talked me into going to a seminar where a doctor was going to explain to all of us boy friends and husbands scientifically why their women turned into monsters several days a month.

I was rather shocked to see a couple dozen couples sitting around waiting for the program to begin. I thought for sure I was the only one to have ever had to endure living around a crazy woman four days a month. It was getting on about fifteen minutes past start time when the leader appeared with the doctor. Only we found out this was not THEE doctor but a substitute. This brave substitute doctor started off the discussion by literally saying he thought PMS was bull shit and he accepted this invitation to shed some light on the subject.

He gave some clinical facts and made a statement that stunned the female audience. He said, "all of you here hold positions in business and society during which never is this syndrome displayed upon anyone except these men sitting here whom you choose to unload on as soon as you get home."

Well uproar doesn't quite approach the results of that statement. Before anyone could say anything, this very handsome younger man stood up and said to this stunningly beautiful redhead, "I have been telling you this all along and I am through with you and your PMS." And he stormed out of the room. Needless to say, the meeting ended. Shortly thereafter I too took leave of The Wicked Witch.

Keith Wells

Chapter 8
Guadalajara

ITESM
Instituto Tecnologico Y De Estudios Superiores De Guadalajara

After my five year early retirement offer at the University of New Mexico I was not really ready to hang up the gloves at 57. I had heard of a couple in Albuquerque who had gone down to Costa Rica and gotten a fabulous deal on some beach property so I thought maybe I could teach down there for a semester or two and check out the scene.

I placed an ad for an accounting teacher on a Central American site and had a reply from Jorge Gonzales-Gonzales within three hours (No, that's not a misprint, it is Gonzales-Gonzales) Jorge seemed quite excited to have a native english speaker to teach cost accounting at ITESM, a technological university in Guadalajara, Mexico. Not really what I had in mind, but Jorge continued to email me regularly for the next month. One day I sent him an email saying that I had heard quite a bit about his program and the goal of having a fourth of the classes taught in English but I had not heard anything about pay or where I might live in Guadalajara.

Within three hours a three page contract arrived specifying

Keith Wells

the location of the guest temporary housing we would live in, the curtesy bus that would take us all to class, the new computer that would be at my desk, the pay I would receive (a full third of my most current salary) and the name of the English speaking Frenchman, Bertran, who would meet us at the airport.

After much consternation, Deb (the trophy wife as friends called her) and I started getting shots and packing for a year in Guadalajara. Bertran did indeed meet us at the GDL airport. He was about half my age and we got along famously. He was dating a Mexican girl and studying the complexities of marrying into a foreign family They did in fact marry despite his hypochondriac fears of "amebas" for which he drowned everything he ate in lime juice to kill the little rascals.

I did not find out until I got to Guadalajara that ITESM was the college of choice for wealthy Mexican's kids. I had kids from the Minister of Tourism, the largest agricultural producer in Mexico, the largest junk jewelry manufacturer in Mexico and the heir to Jose Cuervo tequila in my classes. The Jose Cuervo kid had five personal cars. Numerous times he or other kids would see me walking, stop to pick me up, and delivery me to my destination. We had no car and depended entirely on buses, some of which would pass you by just for the hell of it.

After a week in the communal house, we found an apartment in the solidly Mexican part of town. I was referred to as the gigante (the giant) and Deb was referred to as the guera, which meant young blonde woman. Deb would often get approached as a prostitute because Mexican women often bleach their hair blonde if they want to be recognized as a hooker. When these guys would see her blue eyes, they would rush off in embarrassment.

Our landlady was a sweet old gal with a daughter who spoke perfect English. The daughter was an interpreter for court cases involving Spanish speaking people in the U.S. The apartment was tiny but had a beautiful back yard and a grocery store just a block away. The store owner's kid would carry groceries home for us for a dime tip. Once the locals got used to seeing us, and Deb spoke a little Spanish to them, we were quite well received. One old man would even carry Deb's laundry basket three blocks to the laundry just to get to talk with her. (Or ogle her, I was not sure)

I caught some kids making a snowman in the park beside the grocery store in Guadalajara's first snow storm in 107 years. These kids had only seen snowmen on the flat surface of pages on books so they were scraping away an outline of a snowman flat on the ground. I showed them how to roll snow into balls and make an upright snowman. Thereafter when the kids would see me they would point and say "the gigante knows how to make REAL snowmen."

Eventually we moved to a much more convenient apartment in a very upscale neighborhood. This apartment had a telephone! It was about a three year wait to get a telephone installed so people rented apartments that had phones and the phone stayed in the landlord's name. Funny too that no checks were ever exchanged. Everything was in cash or by credit card. Any bills like electricity were paid for in person, usually by an errand boy called a coyote. (not the people smuggling kind like on the border) Also there was no home delivery mail. We had things sent to the local investment company who held them for pickup if you had an account.

Living in Guadalajara gave many opportunities to travel to Puerto Vallarta, Guanajuato and San Miguel de Allende. Guanajuato was famous for its cemetery which after a time if rents weren't paid for the burial site they dug the person up and stood the body by a fence. Some entrepreneur gathered these up and built the Museo de Momias where you saw mummified

Keith Wells

bodies still with clothes and hair. Seems the water in the soil mummified the bodies. Rather gruesome but interesting never the less, and quite a draw for tourists.

San Miguel de Allende was a favorite for ex patriots who chose to live in Mexico for the cultural experience, great restaurants, relaxed atmosphere or the reasonable cost of retirement there. It has a central tree lined park where locals and tourists alike gather. If you are into art, this is the place for you.

Guadalajara is a very interesting place to live. The downtown area is dominated by a huge cathedral with two spiral towers. Behind the cathedral is a huge open plaza upon which numerous cultural events take place and where families bring their kids to run and play. Chasing pigeons was a kid's favorite game. At the back of this plaza was the Ballet Folclorico where groups from different areas and cultures put on this fabulous colorful show. I always felt safer in downtown Guadalajara than I did in downtown Albuquerque.

As our year drew to a close, Jorge was very anxious to have me return to teach. After all, I single handedly made up a quarter of his English only course quota. He went so far as to offer Deb a paid Master Degree program if she (and I, of course) would teach one year for every year it took her to finish the master's degree. That would have meant about a six year commitment from us. She was quite excited, I was not. I was ready to retire and play.

Individually the students there were very pleasant. Collectively they were a pain in the ass. They cheated constantly until I started putting letters in their file. Three letters and you were out. Other teachers were afraid they would lose their job if they challenged the rich folks kids. I couldn't have cared less; if they fired me I'd go play with the rest of the Americans living there. I was the only one I knew who was working. Jorge told me that I had ended the cheating in ITESM since other teachers saw me clamp down on it with no repercussions so they were no longer afraid to do it too.

On my last weekend Jorge took us to a Sunday brunch at a very swank hotel. As a parting gift I gave him two glass encased Cuban cigars. I thought the man was going to cry. $68 for two cigars was way over what the Dean of Business at ITESM could afford. We gave Jorge assurances that we would give returning serious consideration, tho I knew it was not to be. Divorce was looming for us, not a return to ITESM in Guadalajara.

Keith Wells

Chapter 9
Tucson

Jeep Tour Guide

With fall approaching in Tucson any further motor home trips this year were out of the question. What to do? So I answered an ad for a Jeep trip guide. Who would have thought there would be a nineteen page test!

I was given a book of photos, Arizona history, and geography of the area to study for as long as I needed to be able to take the test. I'd lived in the desert Southwest for many years so most of the plant identification was simple. The history was also pretty familiar with all my Civil War books I had studied. As soon as I got the Arizona geographic details down I took the test and was ready for several test runs on actual Jeep trips. All dressed up in my cowboy boots and western hat, I drove but a seasoned guide showed me the ropes.

The first trip was a piece of cake. I had done a lot of jeeping when I lived in Colorado so keeping the tires on a high spot over rocky terrain wasn't foreign to me. We were in the foot hills southwest of town and the terrain was not really steep or rocky. However, we had to give up using that trail because coyotes were taking pot shots at our white and green jeeps while they

Keith Wells

were smuggling Mexicans into Arizona. Seems our jeeps were a similar color to the Border Patrol and they didn't want us around confusing them. The amount of discarded trash left behind was already becoming a major problem and this was fifteen years before the real issues arose.

Our alternate, and later main, route was much more challenging. This was in the mountains and quickly got into much steeper, rocky trails. Our trail boss taught me how to drive thru this twisting rocky path where at one point you had to ease the Jeep's right front tire to slowly drop onto a rock about three foot below. Guests would usually scream, then clap when you made it safely through. One Japanese woman offered a guide $100 to take her back to the hotel. He had to decline since her company paid the fare to "educate them."

A ways up the mountain was a stop off place where we would circle the jeeps for a little flora and fauna show. The trail boss would point out certain cactus or brush, note types of rock formations and petroglyphs. Then he would drag out the ice chest for the main event. Inside was a snake named Jinks and a tarantula with no name. I mean, why bother naming a tarantula?

Jinks was a gopher snake, but he had the markings of a diamond back rattle snake. He was fed a live mouse per week. In one last defiant move, a mouse had bitten Jinx's tongue off. Since they use the tongue to find food you had to hold a live mouse right up to his nose so he could swallow it whole. Thus the name Jinx.

Gopher snakes are constrictors. One day as the trail boss was showing Jinx off, a lady fell. The trail boss said, "here, hold Jinx." I had never touched a snake before and never had the urge. When you first took him out of the cooler, being cold blooded he just sort of laid there. But Jinx was plenty warm now and he starts wrapping his tail end around my left arm. As I am unwrapping the left arm, his front end is wrapping the other arm. I was most happy to pass this creature back.

The unnamed tarantula was used to sit on top of men's bald heads for very memorable picture taking. I was aware they COULD bite, but this one never did and I don't know why. I guess he was used to the drill. I never touched him, but you had to be careful with him. Their bodies are quite fragile so dropping him would likely kill him and there goes half the show. No one was about to train a new tarantula.

My most memorable and least favorite trip was a trip that had so many people we had to participate the trip with a rival company. It was on a basically flat desert one lane trail through lots of small trees and cactus. These two companies basically hated each other.

I had never been on this trail, but we were instructed to just follow the Jeep ahead of you. Unfortunately I was to follow a competitor's Jeep. At one point he sped up considerably and I lost track of him, but it was a one lane road. What could go wrong?

Well what DID go wrong was that we came to a fork in the road. The genius that sped ahead had pointed the direction arrow to the wrong road. We were on our way back and supposed to join the group.

Well we just got farther and farther behind until I had to stop and tell my four younger passengers that I was lost. They took it pretty well, but were upset that they were missing a cocktail party. One smart ass asked if he could call a cab.

I saw some power lines, so I followed them in the opposite direction of the mountains. This eventually led us to the main road. Tips were pretty sparse and that incident lead to the end of my winter job. My fragile ego wouldn't take that kind of abuse, so I quit. It was nearly time to start another motor home trip anyhow.

Keith Wells

Living Under a Bridge in Tucson

When I left Albuquerque for retirement in Tucson, I was out of touch with family and friends while I searched for an apartment, got everything moved in, and set up a phone and internet service.

Once I got settled I thought it would be fun to send out a tongue in cheek email to all the people on my email contacts list.

I told them that I finally had arrived in Tucson and had secured a spot to under a bridge near a bar named Chuy's that had free food served with booze during happy hour.

I said I was well respected under the bridge by my neighbors because I had the largest piece of cardboard to sleep on. I was also the only one with a retirement check so I could often buy us food or take them all up the hill to Chuy's to buy them a beer and they could have something to eat that night.

I got letters from everyone just laughing their heads off at my tale of new retirement. All thought it was funny and very clever except one, cousin Lois Ann. She wrote an email right back with both fear and sympathy.

"Oh my Keith," she said, "I didn't know your divorce caused such hardship for you!" "Is that safe?" "Are you armed?"

She went on to say, "you know you are welcome to come live with us on the farm." (She and her husband lived on a farm near Des Moines, Iowa.)

I thanked everyone for laughing at my story, but went beyond to explain to Lois Ann that it was all a joke to amuse my warped friends. She was quite embarrassed and said, "you devil you, I might have known!"

Chapter 10
Single Again

Treading On Thin Ice

Renee from the Office of Student Retention contacted me for the third semester. She was having problems getting professors or staff to take a student advisee for personal attention to slow down UNM's high drop out rate. The program was called One On One. Little did I know!

I had had two students before and both were mental basket cases. I protested like crazy but finally agreed to take an accounting student from our own program who had a very high grade point average. What could possibly go wrong! Her name was Deb. She was blonde, skinny, looked very tired, and reminded me of one of those female dogs that had too many puppies.

We had a hard time connecting the first time since she could never make business hours. She already had an accounting job and was trying to keep her educational advancement secret from her employer who I would later learn was her ex husband. When we finally met it was at a pizza joint on her way home to husband number two. (Or three? I don't know) She was late and I was rather short with her.

Occasionally she would call with questions on the degree

Keith Wells

program she was in. She had put off taking some of the required courses thinking she would not have time to devote to the homework required in accounting.

Eventually that semester she started showing up at the end of one of my evening courses to meet a friend who was in my class. One night she and my student arrived after a different evening class, and said they were going to the Firehouse Grill for a drink and would I like to join them. I was not adverse to such and infrequently would do so with students. All in the spirit of One On One.

We were just about to order a second drink when the friend jumped up and said she was late for meeting someone. So there we were, first time alone and not on school business. Don't know if she thought I was also a counselor, the second drink got to her, or she was testing me, but she quickly got to her dissatisfaction with her husband. Red flags went up all over the room. I'd had a couple of teaching friends who had gotten into serious trouble fraternizing with female students.

So I became very cautious around her. She would call me for a meeting every now and then usually at the Frontier Grill. One day she proposed a walk. Later on she admitted to planning a divorce from the hubby whom she had discussed at the Firehouse Grill.

The summer session had arrived and she was in one of my classes. There she was, front row, right beside the podium with the shortest white shorts I had seen all summer. If it was done to get my attention, it did. She didn't look skinny at all! First real look I'd taken of her.

Long story short, after I was convinced she wasn't trying to get me fired, we started dating. Much quicker than either of us imagined we were married in Denver in her brother's back yard. Mike Palmer was best man. A fabulous luncheon and great room

As I Saw It

provided by Deb's brother as a wedding gift preceded our trip back to Albuquerque to start another semester. Deb had several courses to go and in both of those semesters I was the only prof teaching a couple courses she had to have.

On our first day back, the Dean asked everyone if they did anything eventful during the summer. When he came to me I said I gotten married! I had been single for six years and this news brought gasps from all around the room. The Dean said "who, I didn't even know you were dating anyone!" I said "yes, that was kind of the idea. It's Deb our top accounting student." You could have heard a pin drop!

I had a meeting with the Dean and told him "Deb still needs two of my classes, will that be a problem for you?" His response was "no, but it might be for you!"

We were so paranoid that other students would find out we were married that we took separate cars to school and paid for two parking permits. Only the girl friend who left us at the Firehouse Grill knew. To Deb's credit, she studied very hard to get high A's in both classes so no-one could ever say there was favoritism given to her.

On the day of graduation when her name was called I grabbed her and gave her a kiss. The student body and guests were aghast. The Dean said "it's alright, they are married." After the graduation service Renee approached me and said "I didn't think you would take the One On One Program quite this far."

Melaque Was Beautiful Nevertheless

People often ask "when did you first realize the marriage was going south?" My first clue with wife #2 was when we were walking along a beautiful beach in Melaque Mexico and she said "I think you should go ahead with your retirement plan, I think I would like to work another five years at least." As far as I know

Keith Wells

she is still working twenty three years later. This was not the plan I THOUGHT we were on.

As I approached 57, the University had given me an option since I had tenure; let us buy you out or we will fire you. Seemed like a buyout was the better option even if I was not quite ready for the old rocking chair. I was however ready for some travel and adventure.

A couple of years prior to that fateful walk on the beach, I was convinced to give Instituto Tecnologico y de Estudios Superiores de Mexico a year as an accounting maestro. I was at that time their only full time native English speaker.

It was the end of this one year that brought me to that beach in Melaque where we were considering continuing our marriage. Needless to say I would be embarking on a retirement by myself. I got rather lonely after we split and decided to fly back to see some friends in Guadalajara. One of them got me a room in a house where the landlady was encouraged to speak only Spanish to me. This friend also encouraged me to come back to live there and enroll in an intensive Spanish language school, which I decided I would do. Various friends were trying to introduce me to several single women. I was quite interested in one of them until I heard she had a husband, so I returned to Albuquerque to ponder my fate.

As that old song "All My Exes Live In Texas" goes, I now had two exes who lived in Albuquerque and it became prudent for me to move on. My reasoning given to friends was that it had become too cold in Albuquerque in the winter. My actual plan was to return to Guadalajara to take Spanish classes and to stay among friends I had made there until the sting of another divorce had past. Since I needed to take a considerable amount of stuff with me the obvious choice for driving back to Guadalajara was VW camper van number three. I loaded the van with all it could

As I Saw It

hold and set out for my first stop, Tucson. There I would cross the border at Nogales and drive down to Guadalajara. That crossing never happened because I really liked what I saw in Tucson and soon signed a one year lease on an apartment with a balcony overlooking a swimming pool.

I had so little time with van number three I didn't get time to name it like the others. Instead I flew back to Albuquerque and picked up my Nissan 300Z that I had put into storage. That meant VW van #3 was to be put up for sale. I listed it for exactly what I had paid, still unaware that VW vans were in high demand in California. It was not long before artist Noel Daggett called and wanted a test drive. I figured he was a struggling artist since a well known one wouldn't be buying a well used VW van for $2,500. I was later told that Noel had painted a mural in the Coast Guard Academy. Whether that was true or not I really don't know.

When I drove over to Noel's house for his test drive he asked me to drive while he rode shotgun. He told me to speed up along this long stretch of deserted desert road, then he said to slam on the brakes. I guess he was convinced the van had good brakes because he said he would take it. As I was leaving he said "now drive back home safely and don't damage it in any way, I'll pay you cash for it tomorrow." I thought, well that was easy, and started on home.

I didn't get two miles and it started missing and slowed to a crawl. I was just blocks from an independent VW repair shop so I limped it over to the shop. The mechanic said it was a blown head gasket and would cost $500 to repair. I could have guessed that. I had a 1965 VW Bug blow a head gasket on a trip from Illinois to Denver. The first VW camper I had, which I named Lurch, blew one traveling to Key West from LA, and now another. Do you see a pattern here?

It was with much in-trepidation that I called Noel to explain

Keith Wells

the unfortunate situation. I told him I would knock off the $500 for the repair if he still wanted it and much to my surprise he agreed. He was planning to drive it up into the north west and on to Alaska while stopping to paint landscapes. When I went over to his house with the title he told me that because of my honesty he wanted to give me two prints. I was rather impressed with all the art he had painted in his home and adjacent gallery. With the numbered and autographed prints he gave me, I found a Barclays Gallery brochure with these two prints listed for $900 each. Honesty pays.

Selling VW camper #3 would not be the end of my camping days. I had another Ford van and three motor homes and would spend much of the next six years traveling and camping through out the western USA trying to hit every State and National Park.

Yacht Club

Since I had two exes in Albuquerque it was time to shift the retirement to Tucson. I spent the first few weeks in the new apartment and cruising around trying to learn my way around town.

Finally I needed some social interaction so I answered an ad for a singles club called The Yacht Club. I thought a club so irreverent as to establish a yacht club in the middle of the desert deserved a try.

The old fellow who answered the phone invited me to a Super Bowl party at his house that weekend. On Sunday I went out to his house far up in the foothills overlooking Tucson. I carried along my bag of chips and jar of salsa, always a favorite at parties, so I was hoping it would be ok as my contribution.

When I rang the doorbell a much older than I expected lady answered the door. She was very gracious and invited me in. As we passed thru the living room toward the kitchen to place my

As I Saw It

chips on a table, I hear a woman's voice say, "ah, new meat."

I was kind of shocked and turned around to leave. The first lady grabbed my arm and said, "oh please stay, she was just razing you because you look so young." I said I was 59 and definitely not young. She said, "well you are definitely the youngest one here."

John, owner of the house, was an old Ohio State football player and had trophies all over the house and stories to go with them. The other male members were all very pleasant but definitely older.

The next week the lady who answered the door called and said she was having a dinner at her house and could I come. I said yes and proceeded over there on Friday evening with a bottle of wine expecting a party. Much to my surprise it was a table set for two! Red flags! Red flags!

My surprised reaction didn't phase her. She served up a drink then proceeded to set up dinner. When we sat down one of the first things out of her mouth was, "if we are to have sex you will have to agree to be tested first, is that ok with you?"

I nearly swallowed my fork, but I tried hard to be gracious. I got the impression the women in that group were eager to latch on the last sex they might ever have, and the men couldn't care less. So I gave her a sob story about having just been divorced and had no interest what so ever in sex or even dating anyone.

When the word of my "virginal tendencies " got out I was never again spoken to in any suggestive manner. That did not detract at all from my popularity in the club once the ladies discovered I could dance. At each event where music was available they danced my little legs off. The men were thrilled as it took the pressure off of them.

I returned to the Yacht Club frequented to kibitz with some of my favorite members. I was frequently asked to accompany some of the members as a guest to a dinner or dance. It was fun to go

Keith Wells

to their events because every one was in formal dress and these ladies knew ball room dancing very well. One of my favorite gals there was named Robbi. I always wonder what ever happened to her. She had a giant poodle dog that was one of the best trained dogs I have ever seen. Had he been able to speak, he'd have made a great butler.

Chapter 11
Travels

Some Tips on Baby Care

"If you teach you will have all your summers off," Mike said on that train trip to Boda, Norway. I had been searching for a career change since I knew the six month retirement trip at thirty years old could not go on forever. Teaching seemed to be a real possibly. Here was Mike with a whole summer off from the University traveling free as a bird. With a little help from a teacher incentive scholarship grant and some left over VA funds I became a Community College teacher and the first summer was fast approaching.

We had a choice: Nova Scotia or Alaska. Although Nova Scotia had a real draw for me and it was a fourth the distance, we packed up the new Plymouth Fury and headed to Alaska. Quite an undertaking since we had to have a playpen and a sea bag full of disposable diapers for our nine month old son Scott. The in-laws had given up trying to lecture me on prospective travel plans after our six months long early retirement trip. I did concede to stop in Chicago to see them just before heading north into Canada.

A typical over night camping stop for us would be to drag

Keith Wells

the playpen off the rooftop carrier, the set it up with Scott safely contain, or shall we say corralled inside. Mosquitos were a problem so we would lather Scott up with bug repellent at every stop, then set about getting all the camping cookware out of the aluminum trunk we carried on the roof top carrier alongside the playpen.

We stopped at Banff in Alberta to camp near the beautiful Lake Louise with its turquoise water and soaring mountains beyond. Although the campground near Banff seemed considerably more remote than Jasper, Jasper would produce our first bear encounter. He was not that big but nevertheless managed to terrorize the campers for a while. I wasn't sure why the people down the way from us were so concerned, we were the ones sleeping in a pup tent.

British Colombia was spectacular and we followed a railroad track through spectacular mountain scenery to Prince Rupert where we boarded a car ferry for Haines, Alaska which wandered up through Ketchikan, Sitka, Juneau, and Wrangell to Haines. Scott was not walking yet so we didn't have to worry about him stepping off the ferry, but we did have to keep a constant eye on him. His most mentionable moment was when he decided it was lunch time and yanked Carol's sweat shirt up. I thought the old guy watching us would have a cardiac over it.

From Haines we had about 300 miles of gravel road in route to Anchorage. It was on that road at a very deserted campsite that we encountered our second bear. He was quite enthralled with a trash bin across the campground from us, so he didn't present any problem except for a sleepless night in fear he might return. The gravel road was a bit much for our new Plymouth. We had to replace all four of the flimsy tires they put on new cars in the mid 1970's.

It took twenty days to reach Anchorage and we were blessed

to have college friends, Jim & Elrita, living there who opened their home to us every couple of weeks to get reorganized. We nearly killed them though on a trip down to Seward on a rail car that ferried automobiles. Seems pretty dangerous now thinking back on it but you stayed in your car while the train took you southbound. As we were sitting there chatting the Plymouth started to rock! It was bouncing so much that I really believed it would jar the car loose from its chained position and catapult us off the train car bed. At very least it might cause our poor hostess to miscarry their first child. Thankfully that didn't happen, but now we realized that gravel road caused the car to need all new shocks as well as new tires.

Mt McKinley (now Denali) was totally covered by clouds that first night when we got to the campground. It would prove to be an exciting night. Some crazy girls down from us decided the middle of a forest, in bear country, would be the perfect place to fry bacon! Why not hang raw meat on your tent! The girls threw the bacon grease into a dumpster about fifty foot from our tent. About one in the morning I hear footsteps outside the tent. I peeked out a vent window in the tent and saw this huge bear walking between our tent and our car. He ignored us and headed for the bacon treat in the dumpster on the other side of the car. I woke Carol and we three slipped into the car. After the bear left the camp we folded up the tent and went to different campground.

When we got up next morning there was Mt McKinley in full glory. We took a tour into McKinley National Park. While riding along in a tour bus, we saw a grizzly bear running along a long trail. The guide in that old school bus we were riding in said grizzlies can run thirty five miles per hour. I began to question the wisdom of tent camping in Alaska with a baby. We learned some other camping with a baby tips. Don't set your baby on the

Keith Wells

grass near a fireplace grate; it takes forever to wash off soot. Don't trust large dogs around your baby; a sled dog on display lunged at Scott. Do believe BE AWARE, BEARS IN THE AREA signs, and maybe rethink a two and a half month camping trip in a pup tent with a baby.

I was busy taking pictures on a stop on the tour when I looked up and saw Scott standing up. He was teetering a bit, but I took pictures of his first steps there in beautiful McKinley Park. We were on the road south from the Park when I spotted the perfect fishing spot. I pulled off the road and climbed down to this prime spot. I had just caught a really nice sized steelhead trout when I looked back upstream over my shoulder and saw our fourth bear encounter, not counting the running grizzly. He was a really huge sucker, but he was sitting on his butt, mid stream snagging and eating fish. I hollered "start the car" and shinnied up the bank with our dinner in a net. The bear would not be eating this one, but he seemed oblivious. He was still sitting there eating when we sped off.

Our hosts took us up to one of their parents' cabins over a week end. Those hearty folk loved running out of a 120 degree sauna and jumping into this freezing cold lake. Damn!Talk about shivering and shriveling! This cabin was located in a very remote area with only a few other cabins anywhere to be seen. However, the parents were building across the lake, accessible only by boat, to get to a "spot more secluded." As we were standing there on the building site, I looked down at my Levis. The blue was just barely visible because they were absolutely covered in mosquitoes. Good that we had lathered up Scott with repellent. Scott learned another lesson in the remote cabin, do not put your hand on a hot, room heating stove. Poor little guy.

The trip back across the U.S. was uneventful, thankfully. We had to laugh tho driving through Nebraska we caught ourselves

As I Saw It

looking expectantly around the edge at every tree lined lake for a grazing moose. Some habits are really easy to adapt.

Traveling With Lurch

I wasn't exactly unhappy selling real estate at Boulder Realty across the street from the park where hippies gather every day after noon to commune. I especially liked the rather attractive couple that were convinced no one could see them copulating across the street about 75 feet from my desk. She, I thought, was particularly attractive but was by many Boulder residents called a "dirty hippy." She didn't look a bit dirty to me. A bit promiscuous perhaps, but definitely not dirty. But then I WAS only 29 at the time. A shrub with a lingerie draped over it blowing in the wind would look good.

A vacation to Yellowstone National Park presented a chance meeting that would change our future considerably. Carol and I pulled up to a site called the mud flats where there was a board walk out over the hot mud where you could walk out and watch the mud bubble up. We were sitting there on the curb changing our sandals to tennis shoes when a big newer Chrysler New Yorker pulls up and two old obviously retired couples got out to view the scenery. One of the old gentlemen said to the other "come on Harry let's walk out on the boardwalk." Poor old Harry said, "oh my, I'd like to but I don't think I can walk a quarter of a mile." This confession worked on my mind for weeks and months to come.

A newcomer to real estate sales in Boulder was a rough row to hoe. Most of the sales went to several really well known individuals in the community. One was a very popular university athlete. Hard to complete with that recognition, so I had a lot of free time on my hands. Often I would take long lunches with a buddy named Mike. On more than one occasion we talked of

Keith Wells

the unfairness of old Harry not being able to walk a quarter of a mile to enjoy that retirement he'd worked so long to achieve. We talked of how nice it would be to take a retirement trip when you were 29 instead of having to wait until you were too old to enjoy it.

Mike kept egging me on saying if it bothers you that much do it! It took six months to convince myself and then Carol to do a retirement trip at now 30 years old. Her family came unglued. "Are you nuts! You are not even 30 and you think you can retire!" Even her 14 year old brother lectured me. Only the old maiden aunt told me "You do what ever you want, I think it's a great idea."

So we sold a house, quit two jobs, sold two cars and bought a three year old Volkswagen camper that we named Lurch. I wouldn't say Lurch was the slowest thing on the road, but it came really close. The trip started by storing our household stuff in Mike's crawl space followed by a meandering route down through New Mexico, across Arizona and eventually into California. While in LA we toured the Queen Mary. As we stood on deck I said to Carol, "Wouldn't it be great to just continue this on to Europe?" She just sort of looked at me as though I had lost all touch with reality.

The destination plan was Key West, and as we made our way east a stop in Carlsbad Canyon was planned where Mike and his wife were meeting us in their Ford camper van that I had previously sold to him. After our meeting with the customary handshake and hugs, the first thing out of Mike's mouth was, "We're going to Europe this summer, why don't you join us." All we needed were passports which we got in person in DC! Who knew you could do that in one day! Mike took care of the preliminary reading up on the 13 countries he wanted to visit, the "Europe on $5 a Day" book, and buying our European rail passes which more than once proved to be invaluable when rooms were not to be had in the town we were visiting.

Since we had left Boulder in March, the entire trip had spring weather. Desert flowers in bloom in Arizona and New Mexico, blue bells in bloom in Texas and magnolias in bloom in New Orleans. Visiting stately antebellum plantation homes in Louisiana was only bested by meeting Warren and Corless. Warren had given up a Wall Street job, bought a new Volkswagen camper and hit the road two years previously. He had picked up Corless as a hitch hiker in Ohio as he was making his way to Alaska. She joined him and they made a living on the road. She said in Alaska she worked as an exotic dancer and really had to shake her butt off 'cause she had no boobs.'

It was fun watching them have dinner. They would spread a white tablecloth over the battered picnic table, adorn it with a candelabra and open a chilled bottle of wine. Warren would be dressed in dress slacks and long sleeved shirt with Corless in a white floor length linen sarong. There we sat in shorts and sandals sipping beer out of a can while sitting on a log. Warren kept telling me, if you can do this for a year you will never go back to work.

The trip up to Bar Harbor continued the spring weather the entire trip. The Blue Ridge Mountains were spectacular with radiant dogwoods everywhere. In New Jersey the azaleas were in full bloom, I see why they call it the garden state. We had picked up our passports in DC and were headed down to Rochester, NY after leaving Bar Harbor. We would miss Maine. Never again would we have lobster at a roadside table where you selected your live dollar a pound lobster from a horse tank.

In Rochester, friends stored Lurch for three months. They took us to the airport where we flew into JFK and met Mike and his wife and started the second half of our six month retirement trip at thirty years old. Being good with numbers, I kept a mental

Keith Wells

log of the total price of the entire six months including buying and reselling the camper, rail tickets, airline tickets, food and hotels. I can see you calculating in your mind now, but you won't even come close - $3,100. We couldn't have stayed home for that!

When we finally got Lurch back to Boulder, Carol went into the pharmacy where she worked and her old boss asked if she could start right away. I strode into Boulder Realty and my name plate was still on my old desk. The broker said, "there's a couple who want to see some property up in the mountains this afternoon, could you run them up?" Within a week it was as though we had never left. Maybe Warren was right.

Second Half of My Early Retirement Trip

Boarding Icelandic Airlines in JFK was something different. We weren't expecting luxury with the cheap fare we had gotten but walking across a tarmac with no jetway was something altogether new.

There was a two hour fuel stop in Reykjavik, Iceland which seemed altogether reasonable since it WAS their base, but three o'clock in the morning and light as day seemed a bit much. We did get a bunch of yarn in a store at the airport since the ready made sweaters were far too expensive. That was sent home, and Carol later knitted me the neatest sweater I have ever owned.

Our mid-morning arrival in Luxembourg was really exciting. It was the first glimpse of Europe for all of us. The old buildings, viaducts and bridges were really something. Mike had some how booked two nights in a hotel. This would be the only reservations we had for the whole summer. We had Euro-rail passes so we moved from city to city trusting Mike and his $5.00 a day book to lead us to cheap but clean rooms. All but two were bath down the hall type of hotels and pensions. Our cheapest night was $3.50 and the most expensive was the two at $15.50. We were quite put out at the $15.00 ones because the usual was $5.00 to $9.00 per night.

A high speed train took us to Amsterdam. I was amazed by the number of bikes, the quality of the beer, and the houses with flirting prostitutes all over this one street. When we were down by the train station I saw a sign saying "Wall Drug South Dakota 5,357 miles."

We took a train to Paris and stayed at the Luxembourg Hotel on the Left Bank, a sort of bohemian, or student, section of Paris. In the hotel the bathroom was so small I could not sit on the toilet without leaving the door open a bit. I guess they didn't get many six footers. Traveling then in 1971 was not like now. You could walk around freely without hordes of people. We walked up close enough to touch the Mona Lisa, but of course we did not. We were at the Rodin Museum looking at some outdoor art. Photos were not allowed but we bribed a guard with a pack of Luckies we had brought from the States for just such a use.

We boarded a train from Normandy to Barcelona. I bought a suede leather jacket and some European looking clothes so we could look not so touristy. It worked because standing in line at a bank two tellers were making fun of some "ugly Americans" in full Texas regalia. Our teller was embarrassed when he saw my passport. I told him, "oh no offense, those are not really Americans they are Texans." It took him a few seconds, then he laughed. I guess in retrospect we were ugly tourists too, we would be cooling our feet in Trevi Fountain in Rome in just a few weeks.

We were in an enclosed train car with one Frenchman who didn't utter a word for two hours. Then after he had sized us up, he suggested we go to Le La Vondue on France's south coast. He even gave us the name of a friend who rented rooms. This was such a pleasant, quiet, laid back, non-tourist destination and we

Keith Wells

loved it.

We kind of were worried about Rome because it is so large, but the $5.00 book came through for us with a very reasonable room. I believe this is where Mike tried out the bidet - on his feet! We wanted to spend more time in Rome but the madam said, "oh no, unpossible!"

As we worked our way up through Italy, we stayed at Florence and Venice. I loved Florence. Palazzo Vecchio had a fantastic restaurant and the Accademia Gallery had the original David by Michelangelo. Again, back then we could walk right up to the David and there were the only four of us in the room until two giggly girls arrived. One was looking right up at David's crotch and said, "boy, that was a hell of a man!" Then she realized we heard her. She blushed, and ran out the door.

Venice was spectacular. St. Marks Square had three outdoor restaurants and probably not over a hundred people on the whole square. Mike and I met there about 45 years later while he was teaching in Italy. I was so glad I got to see Venice before it became so crowded and such a tourist trap.

Switzerland was very scenic. A pension in Iselvault had an alphorn which sounded like a tug boat when we first heard it. At dinner that night some guy got Carol to dance a couple of dances. I guess it's expected to buy a lady a drink after any dance. He bought her a couple of schnapps and got her blitzed.

When we arrived in Zermott via cog rail we were disappointed because it was totally fogged in so we couldn't see the Matterhorn. The town was wonderful and there were no cars allowed in town. What a delight. When dinner was served, my pork chop had a house fly baked right into the top of it. I knew Margot would have a hizzy fit, so I sliced a little square around it and covered it up with trimmings. I didn't mention it to anyone, we didn't want to be ugly Americans. I might not be so gracious today. When we

As I Saw It

walked outside next morning there was The Matterhorn bathed in glorious sunlight.

While working our way up to Germany we stopped in Mont-Saint-Michel in France. It is an island part of the day when the tide is out. Of course Mike and I trudged out there a hundred yards or so despite the warning that the tide came in at 200 feet per minute. We got some great, and rare pictures tho!

Mont-Saint-Michele proved to be one of the few places we had a problem getting a room. We wound up hot-bedding a room. Carol and I had the room from 10 pm to 4 am. Mike and Margot had the room from 4 am until 10 am. Don't know what they did until 4 am out there, but we ate doughnuts and drank coffee until 10 am when they came down.

We had several stops in Germany. Munich's beer garden was a blast. Some older German guy asked if he could sit with us. He said he had taught himself four languages sitting in that bar talking to tourists! That's a lotta beer! Berchtesgaden was very scenic and historic, but to tell you the truth it gave me the creeps knowing Hitler had walked those very sidewalks just 26 years before us.

One of the more interesting towns we visited was in Germany was called Kellinghusen. Carol had some shirt tail relatives there so we took a cab out from the train station. This old couple answered the door and invited us in. The old lady made coffee and served us cookies. Carol knew a few words of German so she was showing them all the pictures of their relatives in Chicago when a younger man arrived about 45 minutes after our arrival. Carol was asking who he was, and he said, "I was about to ask you the same thing." Turns out, the relatives lived two doors down the street.

When we finally got connected with the actual relatives, their house was most unusual. It went from living room, thru the

Keith Wells

dining room, thru the kitchen, thru the mud room, and into the barn, all under the same roof. The father was fortyish and had an eleven year old son who was proud as a peacock that he could speak with us. As I was sitting in their living room, I couldn't help but notice a picture of two young men in Nazi uniforms on the mantle.

The father caught me looking an embarked on a long, sort of apologetic, explanation of how that happened. He said he and his brother were 14 and 15 years old. Hitler had them recruited into the army, gave them two weeks of basic training and put them on the front lines. His brother was killed on the second day. He said people knew things weren't right with Hitler, but he had gotten control before they knew what happened and then it was too late to stop him. Sound familiar?

We took a train tour through Denmark, Sweden and Norway all the way north to Boda above the Arctic Circle. Boda was having a heat wave. It was 84 and people were in a twit over the heat. We stopped in Trondheim expecting a great fish dinner, but they told us they shipped all the good stuff out! It sounded like Iowa where all the best beef was shipped to New York and Chicago.

We came down to London and stayed at a B & B. First morning down at breakfast I ordered tea. She brought a regular sized tea pot with seven tea bags. I quickly yanked them out, to which she said, "young man, if you wanted water I would have brought you water." When I told her two bags would be plenty she scoffed at me.

Next morning at breakfast a couple sat with us. He was an editor of a London newspaper. He questioned us on our thoughts about Viet Nam. He later remarked, "you know, when you Yanks learn to keep your noses out of other people's affairs, as we finally did, you will be better off." The USA should have listened to him.

As I Saw It

The last week or so of the trip was spent in Rye, England on the south coast. It had been a seaport at one time but the sea had receded two miles away. It was weird to see docks and sea walls still standing. There was a cobblestone street we had to walk up to get to our upstairs room at the Little Salt Coat Inn. Along the street was a hotel with a prominent cornerstone that read, "Remodeled in 1620." The pub we frequented was an operating pub for 420 years.

When we returned to Boulder, the six month trip seemed very surreal. We were both back to our same previous jobs in three days. Within a week, it was as tho we had never left.

Cruise to Santa Catalina

I had not been on a cruise since the Navy days, but some of the Tucson gang talked me into a very short cruise to Santa Catalina and Ensenada. It was on Royal Caribbean. I was pretty skeptical so I loaded up on sea sick meds. I was not the only one, I saw a lot of those little behind the ear patches in our group.

Our first stop before boarding the cruise ship was to visit the USS Midway, an aircraft carrier now a museum in San Diego. It was pretty weird standing on the flight deck looking down when I had stood on a destroyer looking up several times when we were refueling at sea off that same carrier. Their sailors enjoyed seeing us bounce up and down about twenty foot.

When we finally pulled out of San Diego harbor I saw old sites I had seen dozens of times along Point Loma as we were heading to sea in our "tin can," as destroyers are called. It was nostalgia tempered with fear. If you have never been truly sea sick you have missed a very humbling experience that just goes on and on add-nauseam.

I was pleasantly surprised. The sea surface was as calm as I had ever seen it. What a relief. We headed down to one of the bars

Keith Wells

and had a couple of drinks before dinner. Our dinner waitress was this delightful woman from Tobago who entertained us with tales of Caribbean life and posed each of us with a plate of food on our head for some interesting picture taking. I think the two drinks added to that.

When we docked next day in Santa Catalina the weather was perfect and we strolled a mile or so down the wonderfully tropical street of downtown. All the decorations were up for Christmas. Our destination was a museum which when we arrived was closed for Christmas vacation.

We stopped at a restaurant on the way back for lunch. One of their specialties was chocolate malts. Much to my surprise, and her delight, one of the girls had never tasted a chocolate malt! I guess those were not available in Taiwan where she came from.

Next stop was Ensenada, Mexico. I was looking forward to a little sightseeing along the water front, but Ron's sweetie had different ideas. We spent most of our afternoon trudging around to different drug stores looking for some makeup cream at the very lowest possible price. The herd instinct would keep us all together except Vern. He had the sense to strike out alone in search of a suitcase. Same plan, different product.

All was not lost; we found a really fun Mexican bar on the way back to the ship. Not exactly Mexican culture but truly Mexican TOURIST culture. Bring on the Dos Equis!

Healdsburg Wine Tour

If you have never been to Healdsburg it is well worth the trip. It is in the middle of the Sonoma wine region of California and a great spot to stay when doing the wine tours.

I had driven up the coast along Highway 1 in my VW camper before going into Napa Valley and Sonoma. The routine was two vineyard tours before a two o'clock lunch, then two more tours after lunch followed by dinner with the wine of the region. This went on several days before I finished the wine tour in Healdsburg. This cute little town had some great restaurants.

Portland was my next destination where I had arrange to see an old college buddy Doug and his wife. They actually had a home across the river in Washington state. His back yard had a raccoon feeding station where he would put dog food on a platform he had constructed on the opposite side of a tiny creek. In the evenings this family of raccoons would be sitting there waiting for him.

Doug was a big bicycle fan. He'd taken me down to pick up his bike that was in for a "tune up." It was $75. I had never paid over $50 to tune up a car which actually had a motor to tune up. Doug bought a half farmer's handkerchief to streamline his head for $15. Naturally I gave him a lot of grief over both purchases. Some of the road bikes in the shop had price tags over $3,000. Who knew?

Next morning they took me to a coffee shop where all their biking buddies gathered every Sunday for coffee. They were going on and on about long bike rides all over the country, when one of them asked if I had a bike. I told them I had a single speed Columbia coaster bike I rode around the neighborhood. They all howled with laughter!

Undaunted by all that, I went up to the counter for a refill and struck up a conversation with the old gal running the coffee house. She said she loved my bike story. She said, "this bunch can be so uppity."

As we were leaving, this coffee attendant shouted out at me, "thanks for coming in Keith, stop in anytime you are in Portland." Old Doug was really vexed. He said, "I have been coming here eight damned years and that old broad has never spoken to me. You are here an hour and she knows you by your name!"

Keith Wells

Smokin' Up Highway 1

This would be the second of three VW campers I have owned. The first one, Lurch, is still my favorite. This second one was special in its own right for it had a new diesel engine in it. I almost felt sorry for the young lady that sold it to me. Her mother had had this new engine installed and then she promptly died. She said it needed brakes and tires but she had no time to do this as she was leaving Saturday for Florence Italy where she'd taken a job as an art restoration expert. This was Thursday. It needed brakes alright; I took it for a ride and had to use the emergency brake to stop each time. She asked me to please help her out and give her whatever cash I could. I managed to scrape up $2,500 which was just a bit over the cost of the new engine but she seemed very grateful. This one would be named Smokey because when you took off in a hurry it looked like you had your own mosquito control fogger.

Having been divorced recently, (second time) I developed a travel plan to go up the California coast on Highway 1, go across to the Badlands, ending in Okoboji Iowa where I planned to visit my old friends Dave and Ken. A new set of tires and a brake job and I was on my way. Lurch was slow but Smokey set some new records for slow! On big hills I would gear down and creep up the hill in the emergency lane. Most people appreciated that gesture but I still got the obligatory finger some times despite my efforts.

I made stops in Sedona's White Oak Canyon, Flagstaff, and Las Vegas. All was well until I got to La Jolla, CA. I stopped in a rather fancy luncheon place where I noticed a distinctive diesel odor coming from the engine compartment. Low and behold diesel fuel was running out of the line to the engine. What to do! It's a Saturday and no repair services are open. I had intended on camping at one of the beaches just north of San Diego but I had

As I Saw It

to devise plan B. I called up an old University of New Mexico friend who had suggested I call when I was in San Diego. There was a VW dealer nearby so I limped old Smokey all the way with diesel fuel leaking all the way.

As turned out, my friend's now ex husband and his male partner were throwing a huge gay party the next day. I was told that if I would be their professional bar tender at this party I could sleep on their office hide a bed until the camper was fixed. That fixing the camper step was not that easy. The VW dealer would not be able to repair the van for several days. I think the dealer was just perturbed that Smokey had leaked diesel fuel all over their parking area. I wound up having it towed to an independent garage. Those miracle workers had it running in no time and I started up Highway 1 along the beautiful California coast.

But I would be amiss if I didn't mention the party. Huge 20 foot gay striped banners advertised the location at this gorgeous hilltop home complete with a full, separated bar with stool seating, a locked door into the bar, and a window for poolside service. The most memorable guest was from Sweden. He was very stylish and very gay. He floated up to the bar in a fluffy white blouse, extended his hand as if to be kissed and said, "My name in Heh." I kept thinking, what if his middle name was also Heh. Then he'd be called Heh Heh. Or if his last name was also Heh. Then it would be Heh Heh Heh.

First stop was Cardiff by the Sea. Oh my how it had changed. You could not even THINK of driving down onto the beach as we did in the early 60's. When I was in the Navy and had an apartment on W. Point Loma Blvd we used to drive my little Austin Healy Sprite down on the beach. We'd drive up a ways and bury a case of beer down in the cool sand and spend the weekend swimming, eating basically junk food, drinking beer

Keith Wells

and sleeping out on the sand. One early morning I woke up feeling like my feet were wet. The tide had come in and not only were my feet in the water but the water was half way up to the hub caps on my cherished car. Needless to say, we were more careful after that.

Next stop was a beach near San Clemente where Nixon had his summer home. I'll always remember this experience. My usual set up at a campground was to set my two plastic chairs on the ground, raise the top of the camper so you could stand up, drag out the gin and vermouth from my not so large refrigerator and make a Martini. I always set out a second chair lest some fair maiden should stroll by and stop for a chat. (It never happened, but one must be prepared!)

As I was sitting there a couple with a trailer pulled up beside me. They proceeded to set up camp. One of the tricks of this camper was that it would rise to full height from being settled halfway down inside the bottom half. After much trial and considerable swearing at each other about their decision to buy a camper that would easily raise to trailer height, they gave up at about nine o'clock and slept in the thing by crawling in and sleeping on beds a few inches from shoulder height. I enjoyed that scene and slept soundly on Smokey's four inch foam mattress. Some of the best sleep I have ever had was in that those tiny VW campers. Maybe it was the gin!

Next stop was a California State Beach campground near Laguna Beach. While sitting there sipping my Martini I fondly remembered a trip my buddy Ray and I had in downtown Laguna Beach. We'd driven the Healy up to Laguna to have a little beer and sun. Little did we know, the first bar was a gay hangout. (Back then referred to as queer bar). Ray had this propensity to strike up a conversation and milk the poor lad for drinks, then disappear. I had to drag Ray out of there lest he succeed at duping

As I Saw It

another guy out of drinks.

Memory of that event slipped away as I watched this huge RV pull in beside me. This couple was a camping classic. They jockeyed this behemoth rig into position. After much raising and lowering the leveling jacks, setting up the remote tv antenna, spreading out lawn chairs and tablecloths, the very harried gentleman came over and plopped down in my second plastic chair and said, "god I envy you."

San Francisco was as I remembered it from my Navy electronic school days, brimming with excitement. I wandered around Golden Gate Park. Had dinner at Grotto #9. Strolled the shops of Pier 39 and topped it off with an Irish Coffee at the Buena Vista near the cable car turn around. I coached Smokey gingerly down the twisty Lombard Street the "crookedest street in the world."

On to Seattle for a festive birthday party for Connie. I had met this wild bunch of Seattle people while living in Guadalajara. Then down the Columbia River heading to the Black Hills which is considered sacred ground by Native Americans, and with good reason. It is such a beautiful place. I enjoyed camping once again in Custer Park campground. I was rather surprised to see so many motorcyclists. Little did I know it was the famous Sturgis Motorcycle Rally that week end.

I drove over to Sturgis and was greeted by what was reported to be sixty thousand motorcycles. Most impressive was one big old hog Harley which pulled up beside Smokey. This rough looking dude and his fat girl with the triangular leather bikini top looked up at me with such disdain. I looked down at him and said, "you wanna run it?" They broke into laughter and sped off.

When I rolled into Okoboji it was like rolling back the years to 16 years old. Very little changes there except the prices. That $700 lake front lot my father should have bought now sells

Keith Wells

$16,000 to $27,000 per frontage foot. That same $700 lot would be at least $850,000. How many great investment possibilities can I possibly miss!

Finally after sixty some years I would get to stay at the famous Pic's Resort! It was very retro and I imagine little had changed but the electricity upgrade and the mattresses. I loved it. I just propped my feet up, sipped on a Pabst Blue Ribbon beer for old time sake, and gazed out over one of the most beautiful lakes in the world.

I met Dave & Bev and Ken & Jean at The Barefoot Bar a locals hangout that reminded me of Key West. The hatched roofed bars, live entertainment and watered down drinks provided the perfect environment to renew old friendships.

The return trip was quite uneventful except for a stop in a very small town in central Iowa where I was told an old classmate of mine, Kate, lived. I stopped at a gas station and asked the attendant if he knew her. "Oh yes, her husband works downtown in the hardware store." Smokey's approach to the curb in front of the hardware was met with distrusting eyes. My cordial approach to Kate's husband about her whereabouts was shall we say less than cordial. I explained to him that we had been classmates and I just wanted to say hello. I was promptly assured that she was unavailable today, tomorrow and all the foreseeable future.

When I arrived back home it became quickly evident that two vehicles in a small apartment complex was a luxury I could do without. So I advertised Smokey on-line and was shocked to get a call from a young man in Alaska. He was very excited and tried to get me to promise to hold it for him untill he could fly down and get it.

He arrived two days later with 35 crisp one hundred dollar bills. Being in my sixties I was quite unaware that the kids on the West Coast were collecting VW campers like fine art. Yet another missed investment opportunity. Today it would bring between $40,000 and $70,000. I believe my investment failures might be the subject of another story.

The Red Van Trip

I'd taken several camper trips and one motor home trip but never a van trip. I managed to talk Kathy into doing California Hwy 1 with me. I'd been on it several times. Motor homes were not allowed on Highway 1 but there were numerous inexpensive tent camping sites right along the beach. We qualified, tho we slept in the van not in a tent.

Not long before the plans began, I had spotted a red Ford extended window van. Perfect except perhaps the windows. I purchased it anyway at a pretty reasonable price and Kathy & a friend set out sewing grey curtains to slide on wires I had strung up along the side windows, across the back window and even from side to side behind the seats. It made sort of a cozy, claustrophobic atmosphere when enclosed.

The previous owner had already gotten rid of the far back seat so all I had to do was remove the passenger bench seat to make room for a camper type couch that folded down into a fairly comfortable bed. It had to be laid in lengthwise since it was far to long to go side to side. That was better anyhow because it made for a good seat to sit in when the door was open at a camp site.

I then constructed boxes to slide under the bed for clothes and shoes. More boxes for cooking and table setting that would sit by the back doors for quick access at a campsite.

Since both of us had to get up to pee at night, I bought a camping port-a-potty to fill the bill. It sat only about a foot off the floor so a six footer trying to use that thing was a story in itself. Not to mention, I couldn't pee in front of anyone.

Keith Wells

First stop was La Jolla. We had lunch then cruised down to the same La Jolla Cove that I had frequented in the Navy. Same look as back in the sixties. Same gnarled trees, same walkway high over the beach and same sea lions basking in the sun. It was such a nostalgic scene for me.

We stayed in at Island Palms on Shelter Island; a beautiful hotel with a downtown San Diego view from the front and a huge boat docking area on the back view with a ridge of palm lined homes rising up behind it. Cocktail hour was a special event that evening with island music and a view overlooking hundreds of sailboats docked in the harbor below.

The next day was a tour of my old haunts in San Diego; my old apartment on W. Point Loma Blvd, Mission Beach with my favorite pub Johnny's Surf Side, and Pier 32 where my old ship had docked. We packed in a blanket for lunch at my old Ocean Beach beach area, which much to our chagrin was now a dog park.

After lunch we headed to the San Diego Zoo. We rode the trolley all around and walked a few of the bear and cat exhibits. A cold beer stand over in a very Spanish looking area was one of my favorite stops! That evening we drove up to the first of the California beach camp grounds. This would be our first real test of van camping.

I had a cooking box set up in the back of the van opposite our port-a-potty so all we had to do is drag it out, set up the camp stove, bring out the cooler chest and we were in business.

Kathy was a real trooper when it came to camping. She loved it. It seemed to relax her more to see me sitting in one of our plastic chairs sipping a Manhattan than it did me. I suspect it was just having me out of her way when she was cooking that pleased her the most.

I have one picture of me sitting on the tailgate of the van

As I Saw It

with a Manhattan in hand that sort of summarizes our evening cocktail hours. I had on my Arizona Rugby tee shirt which is a bit of a dichotomy in itself. Rugby? Me? What can I say, I bought the tee shirt at a garage sale for a quarter.

We headed up Highway 101 to Cardiff by the Sea next day. The long, steep trail that I drove the Austin Healey Sprite down was now barricaded with highway guard rails. There would be no more driving on the beach at Cardiff.

We camped near Carlsbad so that we could do breakfast in one of my favorite patio breakfast places. Their home fries are to die for. Drive bys in Oceanside, San Clemente, Laguna Beach, and Huntington Beach all brought a lot of top down, cruising the beach memories.

Kathy really wanted to see Hearst Castle so we made a day of it. The size of the thing is shocking, but I was really surprised at how remote it is. The whole thing is a very tightly controlled museum but covers acres and acres of land with the ocean off in the distance. When you see all of this opulence the question that comes to mind is why? I guess the answer would be because we can.

We were really looking forward to spending a few days in San Francisco. For once I had the wherewithal to book a room ahead for three nights at what I considered an extremely reasonable price. We were about half way between downtown and Fisherman's Wharf. It had a Japanese motif with Oriental design all around including a small Japanese garden complete with a koi pond. Parking outside the front door cost me more per day than I had paid for a whole lot of hotel rooms.

It was possible to walk down to Fisherman's Wharf, but not recommended at night. We did walk down several times during the day. Also down to Pier 39, Lombard's crooked street, Ghirardelli Square and of course the Buena Vista for Irish coffee.

Keith Wells

We took the van down through Golden Gate Park and when we went down to Grotto #9 and Alioto's for dinner. A waiter at Alioto's got irritated at us for eating so much sour dough bread before dinner that we could not finish our entrée.

Next destination was Yosemite. We arrived on the north entrance and stopped for a picture or two. Kathy took one of me again in my Arizona Rugby tee shirt. There was snow behind me and I'm in a tee shirt. I guess I was too dazzled to realize it was freezing outside.

Bridal Vail Falls and El Capitan were just as majestic as the first time I hiked back in about twelve miles fishing a lake with some buddies. Kathy and I would not be hiking in as I did in 1961, but the site seeing and camping were great.

Back then, we Navy guys had no back packs so we hauled sea bags of gear up the trails on our shoulders. One afternoon we were "showering" (skinny dipping) in that ice cold water. When we hiked back up the hill to our campsite low and behold there sat a guy and his wife in a campsite near ours. Twelve miles up? Really? We asked them "how long have you been here?" Their answer was, "yeah, we saw you guys!"

After Yosemite we swung down through Yellowstone and had some really fine tent camping. But we were not in a tent, we were in the trusty, water proof red Ford van. Of the seven major treks camping around in the west, this trip ranked number one.

Burros Love Dave

I would always try to visit Dave and Bev in Laughlin during their annual pilgrimage to wipe out the casino's coffers. This particular trip was a winner, but not so much from a gambling standpoint.

I met them at a casino bar where we caught up on the comings and goings since the last visit. I hadn't yet really gotten

As I Saw It

into drinking Chardonnay as of yet, so the order was Bud Light for them and Coors Light for me.

I always loved hearing what book Dave was working on writing now and what was happening in Bev's business ventures. We were old Estherville neighbors but had socialized more since I left Estherville than when I lived right around the corner. Not that I fault her for it, but Carol was not the beer drinking social type that we were.

Dave came up with an outstanding idea, ' let's go to Oatman.' Until then I had not heard of Oatman. It was an old mining town on Route 66 in the mountains of northwestern Arizona. It is now a fun loving tourist trap. As you drive into town the second thing you notice is all the buildings look like the 1850's. The first thing you notice is burros roaming around all over the place.

The story goes that miners left them to the wilds when they gave up searching for riches. They formed herds and roamed the area freely. Some enterprising soul got the idea that tourists would actually pay to see them. Buying food to feed the burros by hand now is a major attraction along with occasional staged gun fights like the O.K. Corral.

We naturally high-tailed it for the bar in the Oatman Hotel, formerly the Durlin, where Clarke Gable and Carole Lombard had honeymooned. Tourists have tacked dollar bills with names or notes on the ceiling and walls for years and years, and the tradition continues on to today.

On the way down to the bar we came upon several burros begging for carrots. We bought a few carrots and were trying to feed the two smaller ones. The larger and more aggressive one bee-lined for Dave's offering. He gobbled a carrot or two and was nuzzling Dave's arm to encourage him to speed up the feeding. When Dave refused him another carrot he went directly for Dave's crotch. In one fell-swoop, Dave used his forearm to push

Keith Wells

the burro's head away, and said, "NOOO!" He then made a dash for the boardwalk to get away from his admirer. I actually got a photo of this hilarious encounter.

The following is an addition from Dave himself:

Dr. Wells, I recall the incident well and every time we go back to Oatman, I am wary of the burros, thinking that the one that went after my personal carrot might still remember me. I believe it was on the same trip that I was going to go up about four wooden steps into a shop. I kind of jumped up to the first step and stubbed my toe and started to stumble. To catch myself, I ended up running up the steps and was going full speed at the time I reached the landing at the top of the steps. Some guy had just exited the store and was holding the door wide open, to which I blasted through at full speed. I recall him looking at me as if to say, "what in the hell is with this guy." It is the fastest I had moved in at least 30 years. There are a few incidents of my life I'll never forget - that burro and charging up those steps are two of them.

Have a good day. Dave

My Last RV Trip

I didn't know it but this would be the last motor home trip I would ever take. I bought an older Bounder 32 foot, class A motor home which looked like a big tan bus. Kathy and I had done quite a bit of traveling but this was to be the coup de grace. Two months through the mid west, across the Dakotas, into the western nation parks, up to Seattle, down the west coast, back through Grand Canyon and then home.

I had a 1952 MG replica that we towed behind to live it up in when we were parked at campsites. We had the obligatory Sam's RV guidebook and a free campsites book. Cell phones with WiFi weren't a thing yet.

As I Saw It

Without the usual fanfare of our departure, we quietly left Tucson. Our friends were used to us taking off by now. The first stop was a jazz festival in Silver City, NM. It was such fun to be able to park the motor home, jump in the MG and cruise the sights with the top down. (The MG, not Kathy you dirty minded thing!)

We made our way up to Albuquerque by the scenic route through the mountains. There we were able to touch base with the kids and some of my old cronies. Then on to Denver and Boulder to visit more friends. The Boulder visit was cut short by some pesky kids trying to steal the MG from behind the motor home while we were asleep in it! After two attempts we pulled out and left for Nebraska to see my brother and his bitchy wife. Kathy was prepared with a couple of anxiety pills. I would need more than that, and it's distilled in Kentucky.

My old home town of Ireton would be next. Ireton was having a centennial and we were prepared. Kathy had painted two signs for the MG with saguaro cactus and "Keith Wells, Tucson, AZ." We were a hit at the centennial parade, strategically placed between two tractors.

We parked the motor home at my cousin Meryl's little ranchette. Kathy was fascinated with Meryl's horses and kittens. I thought for sure we were going to wind up with a kitten.

It was great seeing all my old classmates at the Ireton High School Reunion. There was even a street dance! That was unheard of in my day.

On to Minnesota and visits with Kathy's two brothers. I thought I was very graciously received considering the two scoundrel men in Kathy's life. It's a wonder they would trust any man with her. One abandoned her IN GERMANY with two small children after he was caught having an affair. The other screwed her out of her inheritance after also having an affair.

Keith Wells

South Dakota would be the next area. We were very impressed by the Badlands. What a marvelously distressed looking place. Wind and water erosion at its finest.

A few days in the Custer Park area were very special. That area is considered sacred by local Native Americans and with good reason. The large herd of buffalo roaming the area makes you hark back into what this special area must have looked like before white immigrants invaded the territory.

It was so special to drive around in the convertible MG to take in all of this scenery. On one occasion this huge buffalo passed very closely to our top down car. It really gives you a perspective of how large they really are.

Custer Park campground gave us cause to consider becoming a summer volunteer. You would be given a free campsite for the whole summer in trade for some sort of park volunteer work. My fear was that I would get stuck cleaning toilets like one volunteer I met.

We had a special lunch at the Blue Bell Lodge, a log cabin restaurant that I had eaten in twenty five years before. Nothing had changed, not even the pictures on the walls.

The lakes and rock formations are spectacular. One such formation is called Needle Rock. We drove up there in the MG. When you come around a bend this huge high rock looks exactly like the eye of a needle. As we were leaving the MG failed to start and we had to be towed into town. It took several days to order a new carburetor. We would later find out it was most likely a faulty gas gage and the car was just out of gas.

The campground we stayed at while the car got repaired was owned by this friendly old guy named Rocky. He went out of his way to make guests feel welcome. Every night he would have an ice cream social. I think he just did it just to have people to talk to.

As I Saw It

When we got back on the road, the battleground of Custer's last stand called Little Bighorn was the next stop. It was amazing to walk around and see signs posted on these slopes of where a specific soldier died, even Custer himself.

When you looked at the ridge from which all the Indians descended upon Custer's camp you had to think, what was going through these men's minds as they faced certain death. In a sacrilegious confession I must admit I thought of a line of an old Larry Vern song; "Please Mr. Custer, I don't wanna go." Also a joke that went around, "Would ya look at all those fuckin' Indians!"

A chance stop in Buffalo, MT brought us to a 4th of July parade. All of the dozens of participants were on three wheeled motor cycles. Another stop in Columbus, Montana was equally surprising. We were pulling into a parking spot in a city park area by a lake when an old guy comes running over, "don't park there, it'll be hotter than hell. Park over here under this tree.

Once we got settled in, he and his wife insisted we come over for chili supper. Their kids were joining us. The remaining three days they insisted we join them each evening at least for cocktail (Budweiser) hour.

We entered Yellowstone National Park just below Gardiner, MT. I had been to Yellowstone numerous times but cruising around Mammoth Hot Springs, Fishing Bridge, Canyon Village, the Sulphur Caldron, and Old Faithfull was just different in a convertible MG.

We continued to Bear Lake in Utah. It is a beautiful but desolate looking place. If you are burdened by overpopulation, go there. You'll love it.

Coming down out of the mountains near Provo was hair raising. Any grade over seven degrees is treacherous in an old RV without air brakes. This was eight degrees. I slipped down

Keith Wells

the mountain as slowly as I could to the chagrin of all those impatient drivers behind me.

When we settled in Cedar City two problems befuddled us. First thing to happen was the motor home engine was missing like crazy. The campsite owner knew some young kid who came over to the site and tuned up the engine after he got off work. Such a nice lad.

In a day or two Kathy was having a lot of pain, so I took her to an emergency room in the MG. They admitted her to the hospital. Seems she had an intestinal blockage. It was not her first such incident. Cedar City was not equipped to do a surgery like that plus Kathy was in constant care of a kidney doctor in Tucson since she had a kidney transplant.

The option was to drive to Las Vegas or back to Tucson. The decision was made to go back to Tucson and abort the remainder of our trip. I packed up the camper, hooked up the MG and we pulled out of Cedar City at about 4:00 p.m. I drove all night long through wind and rain and finally arrived in Tucson at 8:00 a.m. next morning.

The plan was for her girl friend Pat to take her to the hospital that morning. I was exhausted and went over to my townhouse to sleep a while. When I woke up and checked on her, she and Pat were cleaning house and going to go shopping. I took this to mean the whole thing was faked to abort the trip. Who knows, but the uproar that ensued split us up.

The question of whether it was faked or a real emergency that corrected itself shall remain a mystery. We did remain friends but never traveled together again and several years later Kathy died of kidney failure. RIP my friend and fellow camper.

As I Saw It

Keith Wells

Chapter 12
Life Changing Decision

Accounting? Really?

Soon after the return from the European portion of my six month retirement trip, I enrolled in a community college education program with thoughts of administration work. Perhaps working toward a college president position by my fifties.

I was two weeks away from starting class when Dr. Banks, my Masters advisor, called me to his office. He said he had a community college teaching job for me. I reminded him that I had not had a single day of teaching instruction as of yet. He said "just go on down to Denver and meet Dean Harley. It can't hurt anything and it might give you a good lead later on.

So I met the Dean and was surprised at his eagerness of having me take a class teaching Accounting 101. I tried to explain that I was just starting school, and had only had nine hours of accounting myself, but he said, "you were an account analyst at First National, so I am sure you can handle it."

Dean Harley went on to say there was a problem with a student and the prof I would replace had propositioned a female student. The girl's mother had threatened to sue the college if her daughter did not get through this class this term with some

Keith Wells

other prof. He went on to say he was really behind the eight ball - as was the college! He practically begged me to take the job and said he would help me in my teaching and my program at CU in any way he could.

He said "at least take this text home and see what you think." It didn't seem very complex, and I did pretty well in the nine hours of accounting I had as an undergrad. So two weeks later I was standing in front of my first class teaching accounting. Pretty weird since I thought I would be teaching marketing before taking an administration position which was my undergrad degree. Who knew I would be teaching accounting until retirement.

On the first day of class the problem student was easy to spot. She was in the first row with a red skirt about eight inches below her crotch. I never got the impression she was testing me, but she had the attention of all my male students. After a few weeks I thought it prudent to advise the Dean that she was not doing well in my class. He immediately authorized tutorial money beyond my salary for me to work with her outside of class as much as I could.

I did in fact work a couple of hours per week with her, but she failed my mid-term and was probably going to fail the class. About a week before the final her mother made an appointment with me and I feared the worst. However she said, "young man I want you to thank you so much for trying so hard to help my daughter, but I recognize she is dumb as a fence post and if she doesn't pass it won't be because you didn't try." The girl actually did pass with a D-.

The Dean was so pleased with me he offered me a class every semester I was in the grad program. My second class was in small business management for which I felt pretty qualified having analyzed a lot of small businesses at the bank. In my very first evening I gave my introductory remarks and told the class I

As I Saw It

would start the lecture. Before I got started an older gentleman raised his hand and said, "I am wondering what a bearded hippie like you from Boulder is going to be able to teach someone like me who has been in business for twelve years."

You could have heard a pin drop. Fifty three students were waiting for my response. I said, " well sir, with your attitude probably not a damned thing." And I went on with the lecture on financing a small business.

I thought it pertinent to tell Dean Harley what happened as soon as possible because I expected some repercussions on this altercation. True to his word about helping me in anyway he could the Dean called this student in and kicked him out of my class.

I May Have Done It This Time

I had bought this little gold seventy something Opel just to drive down to the new job in Albuquerque. It was loaded to the max with stuff I would need until Carol and the kids would arrive in December.

The drive from Estherville across the boring state of Nebraska and south from Denver was nothing new. I'd done it dozens of times. However driving from Santa Fe down to Albuquerque was a whole new bag. It wasn't that I hadn't been this way before; we had been down spring skiing and camping around Taos and Santa Fe before. But this was different.

I'd never really been cognizant of how the scrub cedar trees and creosote bushes made the landscape look so desolate. I am not a fan of miles and miles of nothing but tall green trees on either side of the road, but this was almost eerie. What had I gotten us into this time.

I was staying with Al and Pam while I got settled in the new job at UNM. Strange that the interview trip was just an excuse

Keith Wells

to visit them and here I was going to be living with them until I found a house.

It had been arranged that I would baby sit their fifteen year old, Jenny, for two weeks while they were on vacation in China. I wasn't prepared for pubescent girl's roller coaster mood swings. She did lose some weight tho. Apparently my cooking wasn't up to Pam's standards.

Before they left on their trip Pam and Al took me to the Albuquerque flea market on a Sunday morning. Culture shock doesn't quite describe how I felt during that trip. There were destitute looking people dressed in rags, dragging along screaming kids in search of a real bargain.

I would drag their Jenny down to the flea market every Sunday just to get her out of the house. Again I was wondering even more as to what I had gotten us into. I couldn't help but wonder where these people were the rest of the week because you didn't see them around town.

The worried parents would email me almost daily to check on their daughter whom I had known since she was two so it wasn't as tho they had left her with a complete stranger. I guess they knew better than I that this would be more challenging than caring for my four year old daughter.

I would assure them I would find her sooner or later. Or I would tell them there was still a little smoke coming off the porch roof but no more flames. She would tell them I was starving her and spending all the food money on wine.

Jenny had an assortment of guys chasing her. One rather cocky guy kind of challenged me. I'd been very explicit about getting her home by ten on this Saturday night. Nothing good happens on the streets of Albuquerque after ten, especially for a fifteen year old.

He said "we should be back before midnight." I promptly told

As I Saw It

him if he wasn't here by ten I would cut his dick off. Jenny was mortified! But they were back at 9:55. Guess he wasn't going to see if I was bluffing.

The worried parents got home just in time. It was starting to get cold in the house and I turned on the furnace. It would almost immediately shut down. No one had mentioned the house had an evaporative cooler (swamp cooler) which pumped moist air into a bone dry house to cool it. There was a baffle on the furnace that was there to keep moist air out of the furnace. When I turned on the heat the hot air quickly shut down the furnace. I never learned about that in the mid-west.

I soon purchased a town house and traded the Opel for a small Ford Ranger pick up. Probably not many women would want their husband to buy a house sight unseen. It was however supposed to become a rental house. Carol still lives in that house forty years later.

A sad ending to this tale, Pam ended our thirty five year friendship because I told her I thought she was listening a bit too much to Rush Limbaugh. This would be my first direct consequence of the rising tide of the right wing craziness.

Insignificant Decisions With Life Changing Results

I have thought from time to time about some of the seemingly insignificant decisions I have made that turned out to have monumental life changing consequences.

The first such incident came in high school when I chose to take a shop class rather than advanced algebra. I did get some very useful practical knowledge in electrical wiring, which I have used many times, but I found myself way behind in electronics school and freshman year of college. In both cases I had to do months of make up work in math. It nearly caused me to lose the Navy school experience.

Keith Wells

The next incident was a decision to go to South Dakota State College instead of Westmar College in Le Mars, IA where several of my friends were going. I didn't like SDSC. They didn't have a program that I envisioned and the decision to withdraw mid semester lead me to join the Navy which matured me but at great expense.

While in the Navy I made two monumentally incorrect decisions. One was to have chosen to be on a destroyer which lead to months of sea sickness. This could easily have been avoided had I had the foresight to study up on classes of ships and chosen the largest in the fleet. The other really consequential move was stepping off a moving cattle car. (A vehicle to move sailors around a base) I broke a wrist in that fall that lead to five and a half months treating the wrist and six months of treatment for a staphylococcus infection I got in the hospital.

Another life changing decision was one to go visit some friends in Chicago while awaiting a discharge from the hospital. That which was supposed to be a few days of fun and games before returning to California, became three years involving two career changes, a decision not to move to Phoenix, an eventual marriage, and two kids! I didn't see that one coming!

One decision while in Chicago that deserves special mention is the one to attend a dance at the Congress Hotel where I was introduced to Carol Weber who would be the reason I passed up moving to Phoenix, and would become my wife and mother of my two kids.

A very monumental decision was the one to take a six month retirement trip when I was twenty nine. It would take a couple of years to get it altogether but we traveled three months in a VW Van then three more months in thirteen countries of Europe. It was one of the smartest decisions I have ever made. It was on this trip that Mike Palmer told me about community college teaching

As I Saw It

which opened up a whole new career.

While back in grad school preparing for community college teaching, a monumental thing occurred. I met Clark and Pat who would be instrumental in getting me to leave Colorado which I never thought would occur. Thirty four years later they introduced me to Becky Selfe. Once again Clark and Pat were instrumental in getting me to leave a western state. Ironic since I love the west.

A very costly move with life long financial implications was to tell my doctoral advisor that I thought his program was weak when he asked my opinion. I got blackmailed for telling the truth. Honesty is not always the best policy.

Another really life changing decision was to take an interview trip to Albuquerque primarily for the purpose of visiting a friend. This led to one of those opportunities you just can't turn down. But the decision to take that job led to changing the family's life forever. Location change, cultural change, schooling changes, friend changes, and ultimately divorce.

A decision that ultimately saved my life was one to dig up some tile in two bedrooms of my retirement townhouse in Tucson. I had need of boxes or bags to scrap the broken tile. One morning while putting a bag of tile into this huge trash bin behind my house, I saw a pile of folded grocery bags in the bin. I leaned over the edge of the bin to pick them up when my foot slipped on the gravel and I broke two ribs. An X-ray revealed the first sign of pancreatic cancer. A clever surgeon cut that area out or I would not be writing this short story today.

Another perhaps not so life changing decision was to chase down a lady, Kathy, who I had been trying all evening to get a dance with. I told her I was so sad to see her leave because I had been trying to get a dance with her. That lead to a four year relationship which covered many miles of van and RV travel,

Keith Wells

which I really enjoyed doing. RIP Kathy.

Again Clark and Pat come into changing my life. When I had the pancreatic scare, they came to Tucson to visit me. Now that I had recovered they felt I should travel to Virginia to visit them. When I did, they introduced me to Becky Selfe. We have been together ever since.

For my last life changing decision, I will recall a phone call we made while on a visitation trip to The Villages, FL. Contrary to what we expected, the realtor who settled us into a house for our three day familiarization trip never bothered us once. On the last day Becky said "we should at least call him" so we did. This led to me buying a home here while we already had my home in Tucson and her home in Virginia.

This would lead Becky to sell her home and leave her community of forty one years and me to once again to sell my home and leave the west. After introducing Becky to the west, the choice she gave me was her or the west. So here we are, FROGS in The Villages. Here till we croak.

Chapter 13
Jobs & Investments

High Paying Jobs I Haven't Had

My first job was Candy Counter Exec. I was five or six years old. Saturday was the busiest day of the week at my Dad's general store so my parents and our clerk, Matilda, could not take time for some kid to stand in front of our glass enclosed candy counter and spend ten minutes deciding between wax bottles of sweet juice for a penny or those sweet-tart dots stuck on paper strips. No, that was my job. Dad taught me to count back change for a quarter which was the common kid allowance for the week. He extended that lesson to a dollar a year later when I was more experienced at sales. My pay for being Candy Counter Exec? A quarter a week like every other kid. As a side note: Matilda was so slow my Dad nick-named his old '35 Plymouth Matilda.

Candy sales would not be my only talent at Wells Store in Ireton. I was also runner up for fastest at egg candler. My sister was faster. It seems the local ladies didn't like cracking an egg into a hot frying pan and see a half formed chick splat into their pan. It was kind of creepy down in the completely dark basement with the dirt floor and two bright eyes staring out at you.

My next pay grade was a major step up. Local farmers would

Keith Wells

come into town to get groups of the very few of us "town kids" to walk corn or bean fields. The idea being that while you walked up and down the rows you pulled every weed in sight. This paid twenty five cents per hour, soon to be increased to fifty cents when the local kids said "to hell with that!"

Every year at grain harvesting time, farmers would come into town to hire us for driving tractors for picking up bundles. I was ten at the time. The farmer walks along side the hayrack while you drive. They pitch these bundles onto the hayrack, then pitch them off into a threshing machine. The threshing machine would move from farm to farm. I was ten for my first job with a farmer named Carrol. I guess the double RR made it a masculine name.

My first full time summer job was on a farm that one of my classmate's father owned. I made a dollar an hour doing odd jobs like feeding hogs, cleaning barns and mowing fields. My boss was teased a lot by nosey neighbors that saw I couldn't mow a straight enough line, so it was mutually agreed that I would switch jobs with a farm kid who took a plumbing helper position in town and hated it. I assume he could mow a straighter line as I never heard stories about him. The plumber helper job paid a dollar an hour but it helped that the plumber I assisted was my older brother. My following summer job at Skelly Gas Station was much more fun but paid the same.

I had to take a pay cut to join the Navy, it was $78 a month through boot camp to be followed by $90 a month. After becoming Electronic Technician Second Class (Sargent in Army lingo) I had reached $250 a month by the end of my second year.

It was quite a jump when I was discharged and took a teller position at a bank near Chicago at $325 a month. Seems two thousand laid off electronic technicians in Seattle precluded finding a job in electronics. One day on a medical instrument job ended abruptly when the foreman patted me on the butt and

As I Saw It

said "I think you're gonna work out just fine here." It didn't take long to figure out banking would do just fine.

I thought I'd died and gone to income heaven when a took a job at TWA for $450 a month. I would have liked to have worked at American where three of my Ireton friends worked but American couldn't hire a guy with the edge of a gold filling showing in a front tooth. I wonder how that would work today to have been told that's why they couldn't hire you!

After about eight years of banking, real estate sales, and a master's degree, I began my last career change teaching accounting at $10,900 per year. (i.e. $908 a month).

The biggie income chance eluded me while teaching at the University of New Mexico. I was recruited to teach some on-line courses that the University was making for an on-line college program in Denver. I would be recorded by two camera men in an actual live class.

Tapes of the class were forwarded to the Denver program which aired them on hundreds of TV stations around the USA. My first airing had 32 students. The second had 80. The projection for the next fall would be close to eight hundred and I was to be given two full time assistant graders.

I had students from all over the US from Florida to Alaska. The Denver facility was going to pay me so much per student depending upon my draw. The eight hundred students would have added about twice my current salary. The University's Business School got hold of this information and determined that if any prof at UNM was making that kind of money it wasn't going to be me since I was one of the last tenured profs at UNM without a doctorate. I was teaching in a community college program within the University. So they forced me out.

It's kind of deflating to hear grade school teachers in New York City start at nearly twice what I made after twenty six years

Keith Wells

of teaching. As Bob Dylan said "ah the times they are a changing."

Buy High, Sell Low

Occasionally I like to beat myself up by reminiscing over the lost income opportunities that I have missed. Okoboji really sticks in my craw. The $700 lake front lot my Dad COULD have purchased in the early 1940's would be upward of $850 thousand now. But what the heck would I DO with all that money!

Many car investment opportunities slipped by me while I was in my twenties and 30's when cars were a big deal. First, a 1953 MG TD in perfect condition selling for $1,700. Current value, about $35,000. A 1933 Cord I passed on for $4,000, now valued at approximately $200,000. A 1955 Mercedes Gullwing for $4,000 which sold at auction for over a million. Three VW camper vans worth about $35 or $40 thousand each now, I sold for under $3,500 each. We are talking a million plus in cars alone!

Real estate losses get a bit more painful. One of my Boulder homes that I owned in grad school which I sold for $27,000 now is valued on Zillow at $1,007,000. Another that I sold for $25,000 is valued at $698,000. I'll spare you the smaller losses but a biggie was a condo near lift #2 in Breckenridge, CO that I passed up for $21,000 now is worth about $2.6 million. Shyste! This is very painful!

We're now up to about $3,832,000 in real estate without mentioning the one full city block I passed up at $5,000, one block off Main Street in Frisco, CO, a kind of a bedroom community to Breckenridge. Let's not forget the five acres I sold in the mountains east of Albuquerque or the five acres I sold in Door County Wisconsin, the combined of which would add about a half a million each.

My other "successes" are more difficult to put a price tag on but worthy of mention. In the early 1960's electronic technicians like myself who were nearly out of the Navy were offered ten acres of land in Australia if they would work there for five years. Wells Fargo was offering a special compensation for bankers like myself to work in Tokyo. My uncompleted doctoral degree would have brought approximately 40 percent more money over the twenty additional years of teaching and twenty two years of retirement. All said, a considerable amount of lost dollars.

You can readily see that my long-standing joke of "Buy high, sell low" was not just a joke but a practicing philosophy.

How Did That Summers Off Thing Work Out For You

The big draw to teaching was summers off and every semester was a new thing. Escape boredom. Teaching was a great occupation for me because every semester was a new beginning and a definite end. Each semester started a new experience with a whole new group of students. Summers off provided more escape from a boring routine.

The first summer off was definitely an escape; three months traveling in Canada, Alaska and the western U.S. No boredom here! Tent camping with a nine month old left very little time for boredom. But it would be the last such summer for about 25 years.

Although I taught Accounting, every Dean of Business wanted me to add Accounting courses to my resume. So evening Accounting courses were in store at Virginia Commonwealth and later at Northern Illinois University, even in the summer. Hard to believe my undergraduate degree was in Marketing and I always imagined myself as an industrial salesman with a travel expense account and a company car!

Soon a second child was on the way and extensive travel with one child was pretty challenging but impossible with two. There would be no tent camping with two kids under five. Summers

Keith Wells

were a time for two money making prospects. Teaching summer courses was pretty much a given every summer, but I got involved in teaching business courses as seminars for small business students. This led to teaching Accounting and Small Business Management for the American Management Association, which did not preclude summer sessions ever.

When I started teaching at the University of New Mexico seminars were not on the agenda but summer courses were. I started three separate businesses also, just for the hell of it: an accounting startup for small business entrepreneurs, a gift manufacturing business, and a home repair business for which I did small plumbing and electrical repairs for older residents in my condo complex at less than half they would pay a regular operator. Most of them could not afford to pay the going rate.

During this time in NM, I became divorced and had the kids full time every summer. So my cushy teaching job with summers off every year became one summer off in twenty six years. Don't believe everything you hear about teachers having it so easy with every summer off!

My First Class Taught at a University

A last minute accounting course I agreed to teach at Arapaho Community College lead to a last minute course I would teach at the University of Colorado where I was in my Master's program to become a teacher. Kind of a cart before the horse affair.

The CU accounting department program chairman, was in a panic. A personnel problem with an Accounting 101 course instructor left him with the possibility of having to teach this course himself or find someone in a week. He and his wife had tickets to Europe three days after classes were to begin. He was lamenting this fate to Mike Palmer when Mike mentioned to him that I had just finished teaching a 101 class in a Community

As I Saw It

College in Denver.

This Dean called me into his office and asked me if I would be willing to teach this summer class at the university. I tried to explain to him that I had only had nine hours of accounting myself and didn't feel qualified to be teaching at a university and didn't really have time to prepare for a course with a different text book than the one I had just finished.

Long story short, he talked me into teaching the course by offering me a TA position (teaching assistant) which is a paid position unlike the doctoral candidates who had to teach for free as part of their program. He also offered me a TA study cubicle in the department. (Much to the chagrin of some of the doctoral students who found out I was a lowly master's degree student.) The textbook was changed to the one I had just finished so no new preps. I was also given courses to teach during the rest of my master's program. I understand they had a great time in Europe.

I was just a tad nervous about my first university course, so I arrived early and was sitting in the back of the room gathering my notes for the first lecture. I was dressed in usual summer attire for students at Boulder: polo shirt, white Levis, sandals and a beard. Just as I got settled an older gentleman (probably forty) came in and sat down beside me. He said "do you know this prof?" I said yes, but before I could respond he said "I sure hope he doesn't require much 'cause I am busy as hell this summer with all we have going on in the theatre." He was an employee at the ticket office.

I really didn't know what to say so I sat there until time for class to start and then got up and walked up to the podium. When I started my introduction, I looked back at him and the poor man looked like a deer in the headlights. He came up after class and apologized profusely. I told him not to worry, I had a real solid interest in summer theater and had tickets to the outdoor

Keith Wells

Shakespeare summer presentation.

When homework started piling up from the class I found his all neatly typed. I called him up after class and told him he really didn't need to do that. His reply was, "it's the very least I can do."

Teaching at Edgewood College

I guess the President of Elgin Community College thought he was making a smart administration decision by a late summer decision to not grant tenure to any of us who were up for it that year. It sort of backfired on him when three of us in the business division resigned on the spot.

Finding a job a month away from school commencing is not an easy task but I found one in Edgewood College, Madison, Wisconsin. This was a Catholic college with about five hundred students. I would have to commute weekly until Carol's contract at work was over just after Christmas. I would drive two hours home each weekend to Elgin all first semester.

Since I hadn't had time to find an apartment, the college offered me a room in the dorm which was set aside for visiting lecturers. I was introduced to the student dorm manager and shown where his room was located. In the second week there was a very noisy party going on in the men's wing which aroused me from a deep sleep. I strolled over to the student managers room and pounded on the door. When he opened the door there was a room full of students, more than half women, staring at me standing there in my undies.

One of the staff offered me a room in her house until December when the family arrived. I felt like a stalker there since both her and her strange teenage daughter kept every door to their quarters locked and rarely spoke to me. My room was so cold I had to buy an electric blanket for just sitting around reading.

As I Saw It

Since I was now well known to the students, they felt free to invite me to a beer/pizza party at a local bar. I thought these little brats think they can drink a Navy man under the table, ha! I didn't know Wisconsinites fed their kids beer from birth on.

Well they tried their best, and even got me to dance a couple of dances with some female students. I don't know what was in that beer, or if they slipped a little grain alcohol into it, but next morning I had to cancel class and go sit in the park to look at the horizon since my room was spinning.

Quite early on in the semester a fellow walked into my room. Imagine a guy with tattoos all over his face, only these were not tattoos they were patterned scars. Apparently he was from some tribe in Nigeria who adorned their chosen kids by scaring their faces. This fellow had a terrible stutter and wanted to make me aware of it before a class he'd enrolled in. Seems his boss, the Finance Minister of Nigeria, had sent him to the USA to get a four year degree in two years and one summer. The intense pressure he was under made him develop a stutter.

Two weeks before the end of my second, and last semester, he came to me rather apologetically and said his boss was impressed with me and wanted to hire me to come to Nigeria to advise him on doing business with American companies.

He said I would have a free house, limo service, a maid/baby sitter, a gardener, two tickets to anywhere in the world every year, and a salary of twice whatever I was currently making. I politely declined saying I was very honored but I was on an educational career path that would not allow sabbaticals. My real reason was that I knew during the first coup I would be in line with the student and his boss waiting to be shot.

Only one other student stands out in my memory; a chubby kind of red complicated girl who never said a word unless she was called upon in class. On a final exam, she shows up with a

Keith Wells

tee shirt with a frog sitting on a lily pad. The caption said, "I'm so happy I could shit." Tho I was somewhat amused, I sent her to her room to change shirts.

When the family arrived the suspicion around me subsided. Madison is a very pleasant town with lots of things to do. When ever we needed a baby sister we only needed to call the girls dorm. I knew Wisconsin could be cold since I had five acres in Door County, but I had never spent any time there in the winter. I walked the three blocks to school every day and nearly froze to death. There was a faculty lot to park but we had only one car.

By this time I was aware there would never be a career for me at Edgewood. Too many times I had scheduled a test on some religious holiday I knew nothing about. And the coup de gras was when I went to the Dean, a pleasant but no non-sense nun, to tell her about some really peculiar behavior of the nun who was my department head. Senility had set in and she had become increasingly forgetful. She would forget to tell me of a meeting, then chastise me for not coming. Or she would tell me about a meeting that she would forget, then swear there was no meeting scheduled. So it was mutually understood I was going to be moving on next year.

Memo to all: You never tell any tales on a nun, even if they ARE senile.

Chapter 14
Thoughts & Opinions

Music Man

I have always enjoyed music and the instruments it is played on. My first instrument was an upright piano and it wasn't really mine. It belonged to my sister and it sat in the corner of our living room. The story goes that I learned to lift the keyboard cover and pound out a song on my own fashion or at least as best a two year old could do. I never found out which of my parents said it had to go, but go it did. It was replaced by my father's pink and grey recliner. The only thing surviving the disappearance of my first instrument was the piano stool which was also pretty entertaining in its own right. It had three legs and a round seat that raised or lower by rotating. My mother kept this jewel to use when she was sewing on her foot powered sewing machine. Not electric mind you, it had a foot plate that was rocked back and forth to produce a sewing action on a threaded needle.

The next instrument grabbing my attention was that colorful souvenir harmonica my brother sent us from Hawaii. I didn't have much more success in producing real music than I did on the piano. I do however remember it since I was now four. My sister got me strumming a ukulele next. I learned several cords

Keith Wells

and don't know for sure if my sister left our house because of that or because of the nit-wit she married.

At five or six I was allowed to scale a ladder to the attic in the room that ten years later would become our first bathroom. That attic was a treasure chest of interesting goodies. I was lectured about not touching Dad's gun or other memorabilia he brought back from WWI. What was not off limits was my older brother's snare drum and trombone. On the drum I was a natural. I'd had prior experience at pounding an instrument.

The trombone was much more of a challenge but it would become my entry into music lessons with the school's music teacher. The first few lessons went quite well until I was made painfully aware that I was too small to reach the fourth position on the slide. In came the snare drum.

Lessons seemed quite a waste of time to me. Tap tap, tap tap tap. Why read this stuff when you could play along by ear. The teacher agreed with my rationale but there was no room for a kid who had no interest in the traditional methodology of teaching music. Plus this shyste of an older drummer would have no part of sharing the limelight with a kid half his age with thoughts of individuality. Drumming would return to the repertoire later when the shyste graduated from high school.

Our not so patient music teacher needed a trumpet player so off I went into trumpet lessons with a brand new cornet. Same as trumpet I was told but cheaper. I played third chair but could never better the two Judys who had first and second chair. This continued in high school until I ran into a clothesline wire and broke off a front tooth. No more pressure on that new bridge I was told. But Mr Band director had the perfect solution, a baritone. Same scale, same fingering, bigger mouth piece. No pressure on the front teeth. I finally made first chair in the high school band. In fairness tho, I WAS the only baritone player.

As I Saw It

Snare drum returned to my life when my nemesis graduated. I was in eighth grade then and the marching band needed a cadence drummer. They had a concert drummer who learned the boredom of reading sheet music for concert use but lacked the forcefulness and the ability to play marching cadences by ear. I now had played three instruments throughout high school.

Marching band music was not by any means the limit of my interest. Country music and blue grass had been favorites on our radio since day one. I was very taken by the Elvis style of guitar music and bought my first of five guitars when I was fourteen. My lessons were self taught since I didn't know any guitar teachers in our little town. A disturbing pattern started to emerge though in my non-school related musical pursuits. I reached a level of performance after which I could not seem to progress so I would lose interest and lay the instrument down for months at a time.

During the years of service time I had little time nor space for instruments. But I picked up a used guitar soon thereafter. A good friend of mine, Rick, was a professional drummer so any notion of drumming was quickly recognized as far above my talent level. Rick did get me interested in electric bass tho. He helped me buy a very nice bass from Art Van Damm, a well recognized musician in Chicago. I liked bass but the combination of working and night school left precious little time for music.

My next acquisition would be a five string banjo. This would be the most difficult instrument I ever tried to play. I spent considerable time and lesson fees on learning the first achievement level, a song called Cripple Creek. I must have over practiced because one day my three year old daughter said "Dad, if you play Cripple Creek one more time I'll kill myself." For the family's sake I didn't continue practice to reach the next level of "Foggy Mountain Breakdown."

Years had passed with only one guitar setting in the

Keith Wells

corner which I would haul out and practice up to that level of achievement where I lost interest. Piano seemed like a good thing to self teach. I could still read music and there were dozens of self teaching books available. I thought I had mastered the plateau of disinterest on that electric piano when essential tremor put an end to piano playing. It took away a lot of the thrill to hear three repeats of every key you hit.

Only a harmonica class would claim my devoted attention. I practiced for nearly a year and memorized about a dozen songs from the Kum Ba Yah and Where Have All The Flowers Gone era. I was enticed enough to buy four different harmonicas. All four are sitting on a shelf awaiting the spirit to move me again. I fear this may be the end of my music career.

Boredom

It is hard to fess up to your short comings but at 82 it is way past due. My confessions are from days gone by, few of these are true today as we shall see. I was always easily bored. As a kid I would get bored with certain games. If we played softball too long I would need to switch to kick the can, or let's roll down a hill 'till we're dizzy.

I got bored with kids also. So many hours with one friend and I needed the stimulation of hanging out with a different kid.

I never liked doing the same thing twice. If I fished a spot once, that would be enough for a while. Or I almost never hunted for pheasants in the same place twice in a row.

Dating was different. I dated the same girl all through high school, but it wasn't that I wanted to. I often said to my fellow students, "we are young, why should we attach ourselves to one person and never experience the fun of dating someone new." But no one agreed with me. In Ireton, after a third date you were considered a "couple." No-one would dream of bucking this age

As I Saw It

old tradition. How many people, like me, wasted their whole high school dating experience on the wrong person.

As I got older I became bored with our town. I could not wait to get out of there and experience something new. The Navy provided that escape. It kept me experiencing new things beyond my wildest expectations.

Starting very early on I was very interested in musical instruments. But I would learn to play them to a level beyond which it was difficult to advance, so I would get bored and switch to a different instrument. I went through eight or nine and never mastered any of them.

Job hopping was another weakness. The Navy kept me pinned to a job for four and a half years but after that until I taught at the University of New Mexico I never stayed at a job over three years. We're talking about 19 or 20 years here of job hopping.

Moving was a favorite. The joke was, if my apartment got dirty I would move. It wasn't quite that bad but I moved across country at least eight times. In one ten year period I moved thirteen times, and I was married at the time! I have lived in eleven different states.

Cars were subject to this failing as well. From sixteen to seventy five I owned thirty-seven different cars. Two of them I had less than six months. I called it car fever at the time. The urge would hit me and I absolutely HAD TO TRADE CARS!

After divorce, the urge became women. I guess now nothing was stopping me from the high school desire to date different women, and I did. Probably thirty or so of them. I didn't see a problem in dating different women just for the experience of some one new to talk to in high school, and I didn't see a problem after forty either.

One of my more trying urges was to change furniture in a house. I would redecorate or move furniture to different places

Keith Wells

around the room which drove Carol, my wife at that time, crazy. Now I live with Becky who loves to do that. There is a new decor for every season! But you know what? I don't like change any more!

I would not change wall colors from pure white any more. But we have several rooms that are on their fourth color. I would never change furniture location, but ours gets moved regularly. I could sit here and go nowhere the rest of my life, but Becky likes to travel. And cars, I don't even own one. I own half of a six year old car.

So needless to say the boredom thing is a thing of the past. I can sit in my chair for hours and not do a darned thing. And socializing! Forget it. This new attitude is called The Glens. Beck's Uncle Glen said about eight years ago, "you kids get out there and travel and do fun things 'cause there will be a day when you don't want to do anything." So when I don't want to do something I tell Becky I have The Glens.

Gardening and Other Loves

I have always hated yard work. It probably started with farm jobs as a kid walking corn and bean fields to pull weeds for 50cents an hour. That coupled with our house and extra lawn beside that had to be mowed with a push mower. I suppose they had power mowers in the 40's and 50's, but we didn't have one.

My first house east of Boulder had a third acre of lawn. I have two memories of the lawn: a whirlwind that spread out the pile of grass clippings that I didn't get picked up in time, and a cherry tree that my stupid dog chewed off to the ground. I have seen that house recently and it looks like a jungle. Must make the neighbors proud.

A house I owned in Elgin had a huge corner lot in which I installed a picket fence. I had a lot of help from my four year old

As I Saw It

as I hand dug fence posts and built fencing. The very last step was a gate. I set my little helper in the inside of the gate and then it dawned on him! This fence was built to keep him inside! He said "Dad, I don't think I like this svence idea."

A house in Estherville, IA had a huge back yard. I spent one whole summer on three projects to cut down the need to be mowed area. The first project was to build a tool shed down the slope where mowing was really a pain. All the neighborhood kids loved watching the project evolve. Then I constructed a terraced garden surrounded by cedar logs. The final coup was to plant a non-mow ground cover over the entire remainder of the back and one side yard.

The move to Albuquerque introduced me to a whole new lawn escape design material -rock. OMG, what a time saver! The first house had a six foot fenced in area about ten foot by ten foot. I promptly bricked in the entire area. Walla! No maintenance!

Another Albuquerque house had a large back yard with a three foot drop off bounded by rail road ties. I quickly rocked off that drop off portion which was no more than a weed patch. My kids were quite amused when I disturbed a nest of yellow jackets who were hidden in the rail ties. As they were biting their way up one pant leg I was ripping my pants off and running for a hose to ward them off. I built a brick oval border to encompass the two trees and a very small area of grass, then rocked in the rest of the back and side yard.

A duplex I owned had a fairly large back yard, but the front was mostly a parking area for two cars. I cut that backyard in half with a six foot fence, rocked in the back portion behind the fence, and filled the front half with a hot tub and bricked in sun bathing area. Ah, maintenance free.

My last Albuquerque house came with a mostly rocked in front yard with a few low maintenance bushes. In the back

Keith Wells

yard I installed a sprinkler system that had drip systems to low maintenance bushes and even ran them to several flower pots so nothing would need even watering!

My Tucson house was a lawn hater's paradise. It came with four low maintenance bushes in the front of the house accompanied by a two car carport. The back fenced area was already completely paved in with paving stone. I added a chiminea (clay fireplace) in one corner and presto, no lawn care whatsoever. After being chided by a girlfriend about a lack of greenery, I bought a huge clay pot and planted a two foot green cactus in it. It needed water once a month. Tah Dah!

Well my successful escape from lawn care would be seriously threatened when I spent a couple of summers in Virginia with Becky. These people are lawn crazy! Some of their lawns we would have called ranches where I was from. What the hell? Becky's property was six and a half acres, five of which needed mowing. I was motivated by shear guilt into helping. It took five and a half hours on a riding lawn mower just to cut the lawn, then half a day to trim.

I thought we would escape such nonsense when we moved to Florida, God's waiting room. Now most of the retirees hire their lawns done here where everything grows like a weed. You see philodendron house plants whose leaves were the size of your fist grow leaves 2 foot wide by 3 1/2 foot long when planted outside! A schefflera in our back yard that was a house plant is now over twenty foot high.

Becky, bless her little heart, loves plants and gardening. Our back yard would make professional designers envious. It is gorgeous and has this damnable fountain that needs almost daily maintenance. Fortunately for me, Becky does 95% of the work - even mowing! Thank God because I am allergic to just about everything that grows out there. But of course all my male friends

As I Saw It

and neighbors are pissed at me because they can't get their wives to do ANYTHING outside. Half of them won't even cook! One stores winter sweaters in her oven.

So for seventy years I dogged mowing and gardening as much as I could. Now in my seventies and eighties it has surrounded me. Too bad I don't have some of that energy now that I expended on laying rock and building structures to avoid mowing.

When Did Health Become The Main Topic Of Discussion

I fondly remember in my twenties when we would get together for a couple of beers and discuss where we were going to hike next weekend. How many fish did you catch last Saturday in that beaver pond that has the cut-throats. Did you see the Porsche Chuck bought? Your hair is really getting long. Isn't it tragic that poor Karen got hit while on her bike. Did you ride that crazy roller coaster down at The Pike? Did you hear Johnny's Pub is going to be serving pizza? Did you hear Pam got knocked up? Did you have fun with all the Delta Sig guys down at The Sink? Could you help me put in a fire place next week? Not once did I ever hear "How are you feeling today?"

I told one of my 55ish friends once, "when you hit 60, the parts start falling off." God I hadn't intended it to be a prophecy! Now in The Villages, Florida it is a betting sport to see how many minutes pass in any gathering before someone mentions their latest ailment. I've won the bet three times by betting under four minutes.

The ailments are many including diabetes, enlarged prostates, memory loss, dizzy spells, migraines, irritable bowel syndrome, allergies, pancreatic cancer, psoriatic arthritis, arterial fibrillation, bi-pass surgery, mini strokes, major strokes, heart attack, cirrhosis, gout, psoriasis, essential tremor, cataracts,

Keith Wells

dementia, hardening of the arteries, Parkinson's, Alzheimer's, arthritis, bad knees, bad hips, cancer, stomach issues and faulty implants both tooth and breast. There are days when I feel I have or have had half of these. Of course at any moment anyone old enough to live here can legitimately feel symptoms of at least two or three of these ailments at any given moment.

I can't remember a dinner party or Mexican Train game night when the topic of health issue did not command a sizable portion of the evening conversation. Why am I reporting this behavior of a particular segment of the Florida retirement population? Not because I think it is humorous, though at times it can be. Not that I have a solution to alleviating suffering in this vulnerable age group. Nor do I think discussing common health problems with friends is unusual or should be discouraged. What I am suggesting is, if you have not yet arrived at your sixtieth birthday when parts start to fall off, fasten your seat belt. It is going to be a wild ride.

Would That Look Better If...

My house remodeling craze started in a little three bedroom one bath house east of Boulder. The in-laws were visiting from Chicago and for whatever reason the whole household had a bad case of Montezuma's revenge. There were people in the hallway dancing on one foot waiting for the coveted bathroom.

When they left, I decided this will not happen again. I was sitting on the couch looking down that long hallway when it dawned on me, there were two back to back closets at the end of that hallway.

I started by cutting a door way in that hallway dead end wall. I walled up the now half closets, wall-boarded what had been double doors, and put in new single doors for each now considerably smaller bedroom closets.

As I Saw It

Now it was time to tackle the tricky plumbing part of the job. A very small sink would be in the left half of what had been part of a bedroom closet. The right side got the stool. It was very helpful that this house had a crawl space which made tapping into water and sewer pipes much easier. Having had a summer job as a plumber's helper gave me the courage to begin the job. It didn't hurt that the plumber I helped was my brother who now lived in Denver. He was a phone call away when I needed advice. His help came in handy when I added a washer-dryer in the kitchen.

The next big project was a fireplace put into a different Boulder home. It was made of metal with a cylindrical chimney that had to be cut through the roof. Thankfully my buddy Mike helped with the roof part. Boxing in the construction, wall boarding and some brick work for a hearth and walla!

A house in Elgin, IL was the site of several major projects. The first project was repainting a huge two story house which had one side that had to have peeling paint torched and scraped off. Twenty eight window sills, twenty eight screens and twenty eight storm windows topped off that job.

Next I installed a family room fireplace. Pretty much the same as the Boulder fireplace except I had to hire a brick mason to build a two story chimney on the outside of the house. I finished off that family room by putting in another half bath in what was a full closet at one end of the family room. Another house left with another half closet! That house then got a full corner lot picket fence to corral our four year old. He was not enthused when he realized what this fun project was for.

The Elgin house also got a complete upper level bath remodeling, and a third bath put into the basement. The upper bath was gutted and completely rebuilt except for the tub. Sink, stool, mirrors, and a tiling tub surround. When the project was

Keith Wells

completed, the whole plaster ceiling collapsed onto the floor! I had to hire a wall boarder for that tricky project.

I took it easy on my first Albuquerque house, just retiled the entire house and redecorated the yard. However, the second house which was a duplex got a major kitchen overhaul. I put in another washer-dryer in the kitchen. This house had no crawl space so I had to run water and drain pipes through a wall, into a water heater closet, and back to the kitchen sink pipes. Good thing I had the brother's advice on how to measure drop for proper drainage. I was more worried about that first load of laundry than any of my other remodeling projects.

The third Albuquerque house was a major renovation. The house had this tacky garage extension on the front, an even tackier rear porch addition, two baths that got gutted and redone plus a huge lawn that desperately needed help. I actually had to buy a small pickup truck to accommodate all the repairs.

I started this project by tearing off half of the back porch and remodeling the remainder into a nice enclosed back porch. Then I tore off that tacky front garage addition and returned the front to what it had looked like before this disastrous looking wood against brick abortion.

Two super ugly bathrooms had to be gutted and remodeled including all the cabinetry. While chipping off some old maroon tile in the main bath a large chunk of tile fell off and was headed toward the only salvageable thing in the room - flooring. I grabbed it to save the floor. Little did I know the bottom had a shear edge. I nearly lost my little finger on that mistake.

The kitchen counter tops and sink had to be replaced and some truly ugly wall texture had to be sanded off and retextured. I have no idea what this genius had in mind when he put that stuff in.

The mammoth "need for lawn mowing" yard would be next.

As I Saw It

I hauled in many pickup loads of lava rock to cover up ninety percent of the grass. I have to admit, it was ugly as hell but I didn't have the time or disposition for mowing and yard care.

The fourth Albuquerque house brought on a sliding glass door installed into a bedroom wall that had been a window. This gave access to a project that created a really beautiful landscaped backyard that had been a weed patch.

My only house in Tucson had yet another ugly back porch addition which I immediately tore off and restored to the original condition. It had two baths that both had to be remodeled and the removal of some of the ugliest tile in history from two bedrooms.

When I met Becky in Virginia, I got a shot at some more bathroom remodeling. I gutted and remodeled two baths in her house. Bathroom remodeling was by now pretty much old hat. I'm sure she wondered if I really knew how to do this when I started ripping out old fixtures.

The house here in The Villages has had a lot of redecorating. We've given the ugly kitchen cabinets five coats of white paint and replaced all the twenty eight door knobs with fancy door pulls. Tacky gray counter tops in the kitchen and two baths were replaced with granite wherein my previous plumbing experience saved us a bunch of money by installing the three sinks and their faucets plus a disposall.

Ceiling lights, ceiling fans and built in book cases in two rooms sort of rounded out the indoor experience. Outside Becky has created a garden paradise around a circular flagstone patio I designed.

It is now a conundrum when I think of all the money and time I have spent remodeling houses. Have I saved money by doing these jobs myself or spent more money on remodeling because I COULD do it myself?

Keith Wells

My Affection for Cars

I developed a real love for cars very early on, 1950's I would say. At ten I would go back and forth a car length or two in Dad's 1935 Plymouth. He seemed to love that old car; he even named it Matilda after his store clerk because the Plymouth, like Matilda, was slow as molasses. Sixty five was top speed. This back and forth in front of our house was great fun until I popped a clutch in it and it became necessary for Dad to buy a new 1950 Ford four door sedan.

I'd been driving farm equipment like tractors for several years when Dad found it prudent for me to learn to drive the 50 Ford. I was 13 at the time. It was fairly easy to drive around the town of 350 people because the town cop was my buddy's dad who would conveniently be looking the other way if I drove by. South Dakota was only ten miles of backroads away and believe it or not you didn't need a license to drive in SD until I was fifteen!

I was driving the Ford alone at 14. I actually had my first date in it soon after my fourteenth birthday. Don't think her parents were too keen on it, but I was not the only kid in town who was driving at 14. Fourteen was a big year for me. The bike was out and a 1949 Cushman Eagle motor scooter was in. I practically lived on that thing. I would use it to drive out to farm jobs which worked out well since we only had the one car.

Fifteen was the year we all were waiting for; the year of legal driving with a learner's permit. There wasn't much left for me to learn except how to drive on highways and how to drive on icy roads. My final exam of that combined condition happened one Sunday when I was in the back seat of the Ford. Dad was driving and Mom was riding shotgun. We were heading up an icy Highway 10 when he lost control and the car did a 360 and skidded to a stop heading the same way we were going. Dad didn't

As I Saw It

say a word. He simply got out of the car, came around to open my door and said "You drive." I became the family chauffeur from that day until I shipped off to the Navy three years later.

At sixteen I got the coveted official driver's license and I bought my own first car, a 1950 Studebaker convertible. We would joke about buying a quart of gas and a gallon of oil because it went through oil like crazy. I sold it and inherited the 50 Ford at 17 when Dad suddenly passed away.

After boot camp, electronics school and a West Pac cruise to Formosa and Japan I was on leave visiting my Mother and Grandparents in Springfield, MO. I traded in the 1950 Ford for a brand new 1961 Austin Healy Sprite. The Sprite was traded for a 1956 Buick Century hardtop because it had an automatic and the Sprite's four speed was hard to drive with a full right arm cast. I may write a story on that mishap.

I loved that Buick with its twin Laker Pipes and seven coats of dark blue lacquer paint. Its cruising speed was 89 MPH. But I would be talked into trading a buddy for a 1963 or 1964 Corvair because he was off to the service. I had the Corvair for about a year when I traded it for a new 1965 VW bug, $1,620 total price. I labored three days deciding on spending an extra $40 for an AM radio. I wound up getting a second market one for $25.

I foolishly traded the VW for a new 67 Chevy Malibu. Biggest clunker I had yet owned next to a slightly used Volvo. I got rid of both within six months. They were replaced by one of VW's best models a 67 bug.

I went through a maze of cars in the next six years. I bought two late 60's Oldsmobiles to use as repair guinea pigs in an auto repair class. I bought a 1950 Plymouth for $50 to haul flagstone to make a patio on my first house. Also a Mercury Comet and a Bell Telephone green Dodge Dart of early 70's vintage. I had traded a late 60's Chrysler New Yorker for the Dodge. I also

Keith Wells

owned a 70 something Ford camper which I sold to a friend before buying a 1969 VW camper that was used on the six month early retirement trip.

In 1974 when I took my first full time teaching position in Richmond, VA I bought a new 74 Plymouth Fury. Nine months later a trip to Alaska would just about finish it off. It would be replaced by a used 71 VW station wagon, one of the few models of it ever produced.

Our next car, having one child and another in the making, we bought a brand new 78 Pontiac station wagon. One of the better cars I have owned. Since we needed two cars now, I added a 79 or 80 Honda Civic. Also a good car, but a bit tight for a six footer.

Preceding the move from Iowa to Albuquerque I needed a disposable car to move in. I selected a 6 or 7 year old Opel. It got me there ok, but not a prize winner. It was soon replaced by a new 82 Ford Ranger pick up. For collectors sake, I added a partially restored 64 Mustang.

A separation and divorce lead to a series of address changes and automobile changes. A new red Toyota pick up in about 1987 was followed by a blue Mazda pickup, a tan 1986 VW sedan named Olga, a white Mitsubishi pickup, a gold Mitsubishi van, a new white Mazda three door, and a white 84 Nissan 300Z.

The 84 Nissan 300Z had to be sold and replaced with a Datsun 280 in order to qualify for a duplex I was trying to buy. Much to my chagrin, a friend whose great grand parents were one of five who originally laid out Santa Fe, NM said "why didn't you tell me, I would have loaned you the money to pay off the 300Z." I became the proud owner of a diesel VW camper in which I made my second San Diego to Seattle trip.

A second 86 Nissan 300Z followed along with the third VW camper in which I did my third San Diego to Seattle trip. I would

As I Saw It

drive this 300Z to Tucson in the escape from Albuquerque. Later the third VW camper would be sold to an artist.

While in Tucson the travel bug hit again, so I bought my first class A Rockport motor home. I would trade the 86 300Z for a stick shift Dodge Neon which could be easily towed. That Neon would serve me well through the following year when I traded the Rockport for a class C Newport motor home. Two years later the Newport was traded for a class A Bounder motor home which would tow a recently purchased 1952 MG replica. It was great fun racing around The Black Hills and Yellowstone in the MG.

A breakup with my traveling companion brought the beginning of my aging mentality and the purchase of a Mercury sedan. I took so much gaffe from driving "the old man's car" that peer pressure forced me into a new 2006 red PT Cruiser. I loved that car but wound up giving it to my son. Becky had a Subaru Outback and we didn't need two cars. The Subaru was replaced by a green Hyundai Tucson and a BMW convertible.

In 2016 Becky and I traded the Hyundai for a white Subaru Legacy. I can now say my car craze is officially over. I no longer own a car, I have half of a car. I could care less what I drive as long as it gets from point A to point B with a minimum of maintenance.

Aging is hard.

Crazy Teachers

Mike, Dave and I had all been teachers. Once in a while we would get into a discussion about some of the crazy teachers and professors that we had either had or knew about and which one would be the craziest. That often included crazy students as well.

My oldest memory of a prime candidate was Maude, an English teacher I had in high school. To fourteen year olds, she

Keith Wells

was really old, very odd, and quite methodical. She had only two dresses, a blue poka dot one and a brown poka dot one. She would alternate days, the blue on one day and brown the next.

The very next year when Maude had retired they hired a late twenties, very attractive English teacher who to the boy's delight wore tight skirts every day. She would sit on the edge of her desk and kind of rock her shapely butt back and forth on the edge. She HAD to know what that would do to pubescent boys! All five of us would leave class carrying books in front of us much to the amusement of the girls in class.

A real gem in the same high school thought starting a fishing boat motor in an oil barrel in the class room would be the ideal way to teach combustion engine theory. It not only brought the Superintendent running in but scared the hell out of half the school and tipped over the barrel half full of water.

I really enjoyed the next candidate who taught history at Wright College in Chicago. He wore a sport coat and tie to class every day. When he came into the room he would do this ritual every day. He would very methodically remove the jacket and carefully hang it over the back of his chair. Then he would pull off the tie and fold it into four lengths. Next he would roll up his long sleeved shirt to the biceps, and finally do a whole lecture in story form without any notes or even a pause.

While I was in electronics school we had a Navy chief who was bucking for Master Chief. Apparently our test scores would weigh into his promotion because whenever we were taking multiple choice tests and he spotted a mistake he would just kind of nonchalantly lean over and point to the correct answer.

The following is a series of candidates that appeared during my bachelor program at CU, the University of Colorado.

Most hated of this group was this crusty old goat who had a unique grading system. He gave an A to any girl, a B to any

As I Saw It

jock, a D to anyone with a mustache and an F to anyone with a beard. The other students vied for a C. He would NEVER change a grade or discuss why it was given. Mike might have mentioned that BEFORE I went into his class with a mustache.

Another well avoided prof at CU required a complete, detailed outline to the law book he wrote in order to pass his class.

I managed to avoid the afore mentioned law prof but the one I selected had his own quirks. He would occasionally tell a slightly off color or sexually suggestive joke. Then he would start this giggling that he couldn't control and he would have to leave the room to regain his composure.

A real estate prof at CU was very easily distracted before launching into a lecture by talking about one of his seven wives. Although this was not discussed in class it was well known he made a good deal of money selling sexually explicit novels.

Are you beginning to see a pattern in University of Colorado profs?

Well there is another one. I was sitting third row center when this new marketing teacher came in. I was watching him give some introductory remarks when all of the sudden he pulls out a pistol and fires it at a girl near me who was not paying attention. The wad from the blank cartridge hit my boot and scared the hell out of about fifty students. Can you imagine doing that today?

There was another prof in Elgin, Illinois who spent half a semester coughing, sneezing and blowing his nose before he discovered his allergy to chalk dust. The rest of his classes were accompanied by an overhead projector. That prof would be me.

The last candidate probably wins the craziest prof contest. Mike had this old guy in a class he took in Washington. Bets were made on how many minutes it would take for the zipper on a certain pair of pants he wore to work its way down. On one

Keith Wells

occasion his wiener actually fell out. He reached down, tucked it back in and continued lecturing without missing a beat. Talk about composure!

The Twenty Minute Window

It is a story well known to men of a certain age, the 20 minute window.

When a man is in his twenties it will occur to him that he should be thinking about finding a place to pee in the next two hours.

At forty, this window of opportunity drops to twenty minutes. This is the perfect time in a man's life. Old enough to realize you are in your prime. Young enough to know there is no need to worry, there is plenty of time even if you are driving in your car.

When a man reaches sixty, the window has shrunk to two minutes. When the urge hits, you had better be finding a john damned quickly. By this time you have learned not to put yourself into any situation where you will be more than two minutes from relief. You know the location of ever john in town and probably have had a little pants wetting experience by now so you don't push that limited time frame.

If you are lucky(?) enough to reach 80 years old you are now living in the twenty second window. This is why you see us old guys quickly leave a dinner table, a social gathering, a movie or a golf round and high tail it for a bathroom without speaking a word to anyone.

You might have noticed we usually wear dark colored pants to social gatherings. It won't show as much if we're a couple of seconds late.

Made in the USA
Coppell, TX
11 December 2023